COCKTAILS

Edible

Series Editor: Andrew F. Smith

EDIBLE is a revolutionary series of books dedicated to food and drink that explores the rich history of cuisine. Each book reveals the global history and culture of one type of food or beverage.

Already published

Cocktails

A Global History

Joseph M. Carlin

REAKTION BOOKS

Published by Reaktion Books Ltd
33 Great Sutton Street
London EC1V 0DX, UK
www.reaktionbooks.co.uk

First published 2012

Printed and bound in China by Eurasia

British Library Cataloguing in Publication Data
Carlin, Joseph M.
Cocktails : a global history. — (Edible)
1. Cocktails—History.
I. Title II. Series
641.2 1 09-DC23

ISBN 978 1 78023 024 5

Contents

Preface

I learned about cocktails as a teenager, long before I ever tasted one. During Prohibition my uncle Frank, a chemistry major, worked his way through college analysing home-made alcohol, also called 'bathtub gin', for safety. He only needed a small amount for testing but demanded a quart. If it was undrinkable he poured it down the drain. If it was potable he pocketed his fee and took home his illicit gain for making cocktails.

After the Second World War my uncle Aloysius opened a taproom in Philadelphia. Men, usually blue-collar workers, came into the bar from the main street and stood at the bar with one foot resting on a brass rail. Under the rail was a tiled trough with flowing water to carry away the tobacco juice that was spat into it. Some even urinated in it. A beer with a shot of whiskey on the side was the drink of choice, the bottles of alcohol and mixers against the mirrored wall mostly for show. Women were served in the parlour behind the taproom which was entered from the side street. I remember seeing a 'Ladies Welcomed' sign over the side door. In the parlour a woman could eat with her husband and children, order a cocktail and not worry about being identified as a chorus girl or loose woman.

Until I entered the Air Force, my beverage of choice was a 'long neck', a 12 oz bottle of Budweiser beer. The first cocktail I remember was called a Spin, Burn and Crash. This was a popular drink at the Officers' Club, made with several alcoholic beverages, each with its own specific gravity. The trick was to layer the ingredients in a fluted cocktail glass. It was set aflame just before serving and downed in one flaming swallow.

My serious introduction to cocktails came during a tour of duty in Bangkok during the Vietnam War. After work, life was one long cocktail party. The evening began with a frozen Daiquiri at the Officer's Club, followed by a long night of gin and tonics. I still remember how they turned a milky blue-white under the ultraviolet lights of Bangkok's many nightclubs.

With the fog of war and alcohol behind me, my drink of choice for most of my professional career has been a very dry gin Martini with an olive. There was a time when I could survive a three-Martini lunch, but I gave that up long ago. Today I enjoy a classic Manhattan, maybe two, on a relaxing Sunday afternoon watching a Japanese movie.

My youngest son, Barry, celebrated his twenty-first birthday at Jimmy Buffet's Margaritaville bar in Key West, Florida, and shares my interest in cocktails. Today, he is the head bartender at the historic 1640 Hart House Restaurant and Tavern in Ipswich, Massachusetts.

This book is a toast to the cocktail, the perfect drink to seal the deal, mark the end of the work day or to celebrate an evening of relaxation, small talk and entertainment, anywhere in the world. Cheers!

Introduction

For much of human history, beer and wine, made from fermented grain and grapes, have been the only alcoholic drinks available. The alcohol content was low but still they carried the kick that people liked. According to some, man led a very primitive existence, as far as drink was concerned, until the cocktail was created. In a way the cocktail is a barometer of just how civilized our species has become. Cocktails are not consumed by tribal groups in the Amazon rainforest or by fans at a football or soccer game. The cocktail is a civilized drink for smart, hip and enlightened people.

What exactly is a cocktail? Mixologists and consumers can quibble about the details but a cocktail is a drink composed of one or more alcoholic spirits mixed with a sweetener, fruit juice and/or bitters and served chilled in a glass appropriate for the beverage. Some cocktails are garnished with a piece of fruit.

The cocktail as we know it is a rather new invention. The ingredients for making cocktails – high-proof spirits and fruits from the tropics – were not readily available in large quantities or at a reasonable price until after the American Revolution. The African slave trade, a surplus of sugar cane in the Caribbean and the overproduction of corn in the USA

Postcard, c. 1910, celebrating Washington's birthday. There is a legend that the young George Washington chopped down a cherry tree and admitted it when confronted by his father, saying, 'I cannot tell a lie.' Washington died in 1799, years before cocktails and their garnishes were in common use.

were critical factors in the creation of the cocktail. At the beginning of the nineteenth century it was cheaper to ship and trade distilled spirits than to transport the raw ingredients, namely molasses and corn.

North America was soon to experience an epidemic of strong drink, similar to the 'gin epidemic' of 1720 to 1751 that struck England when cheap gin flooded the country. But America's culprit was 'devil rum' and corn whiskey called 'John Barleycorn'. It was in this fog of excessive alcohol consumption that the cocktail was born.

Cocktails are the most American of alcoholic beverages and at the same time the most international of drinks. Born in the USA after the Revolution, they quickly spilled over into all corners of the globe.

Make yourself a drink, find an easy chair, sit back and enjoy this global look at the cocktail.

I

The Mysterious Birth
of the Cocktail

At least 10,000 years ago, possibly more, some of our ancient ancestors abandoned their nomadic way of life and became agriculturists, established city states, invented writing and mathematics and created laws to regulate human behaviour. At about the same time they found that grain, ripe fruit or honey, fermented by wild yeast, could be made into intoxicating beverages. The action of yeast on carbohydrates resulted in the production of alcohol, which in turn killed off the yeast, explaining the low alcohol levels found in beer.

Of course our ancient forefathers knew nothing about yeast, but they did observe that if a solution of grain and water was allowed to sit undisturbed, it bubbled and in a short time produced a liquid that tasted like nothing else and made them happy and contented. They quickly learned that crushed grapes could also be fermented into another mind-altering drink. Ever since, beer and wine have been the universal alcoholic drinks of mankind until a method of extracting pure alcohol from fermented grain or grapes was discovered.

The alcoholic content of wine and beer has always been relatively low but nevertheless produces a kick that people everywhere valued. Centuries after the invention of wine and beer it was discovered that when heat is applied to a vessel containing a liquid with a low percentage of alcohol, pure alcohol vapours can be made to escape. The process of collecting this vapour is called distillation; the device used, a still. Since alcohol evaporates at 78°C, 22° lower than the boiling point of water, pure alcohol can be made to condense and trickle into a receiving vessel. The process was known to the Greeks and Romans, but inefficiencies in design limited them to making perfumes and elixirs. Aristotle, who died in 322 BCE, wrote that 'Sea water can be rendered potable by distillation; wine and other liquids can be submitted to the same process. After they have been converted into humid vapors, they return to liquids.'[1]

India, Egypt and China can also make convincing claims for having invented devices for distilling alcohol in ancient times. Joseph Needham, a scholar of early Asian sciences, identified several distinct designs including the 'Mongol still',

A still in Central Asia, 1865–72.

Alchemist with alchemical equipment, in a woodcut of 1599 from *The Second Booke of Distillations*, the second part of Conrad Gesner's *The Practise of the New and Old Phisicke*.

which had a device for catching condensation (catch-ball) within the still; the 'Chinese still', with its catch-bowl and side-tube connected to a receiver; and the 'Moor's head' still, with a concave roof and circular rim for collecting condensation and directing it to an outside receiver. It was probably this last design that permitted a higher degree of production and purity. In his novel *Bangkok 8*, John Burkett describes a similar contraption used by makers of illegal hooch in contemporary Thailand.

It appears that ideas about distillation were circulating freely throughout the Middle East, India and China and in turn new ideas for improvements were carried back to Rome, Greece and Egypt by spice merchants and Silk Road traders.

This issue of where and when and by whom something was invented will be a recurrent theme in the story of the cocktail. This problem will be compounded by the natural inclination of people – or collectively, nations – to want to take credit for inventing something. The motivation might be fame, financial gain, national pride or simply to seek immortality. The fact is that we have an imperfect knowledge about the history of alcohol distillation, but scholars are still working on this issue.

Regardless of where and when and by whom alcohol was first distilled, it was probably restricted to making small quantities for use in perfumes and medicinal elixirs. Until the process could be scaled up to produce pure alcohol efficiently in both quality and quantity, it would remain a curiosity of the alchemists.

The person most often associated with perfecting the art of distilling alcohol is Jābir ibn Hayyān, an Arab who practised medicine and alchemy in Kufa (a city in modern Iraq). Recognized as one of the fathers of chemistry, he is credited with developing an improved distillation process around CE 800. Out of his study of alchemy – the belief that metals such as lead could be turned into gold – he perfected a process whereby alcohol could be made in a device called an alembic. Alembic and alcohol are both Arabic words. The word 'still' is from the Latin word *destillare*, meaning to drop or trickle.

In France the device was used to distil wine into *aqua vitae,* a concentrated liquid that was considered therapeutic. This was a logical assumption since the ancient Greeks and Romans

Sikh school watercolour of a man distilling liquid and a man drinking,
19th century, album leaf from India.

had praised wine for its medicinal qualities. It was only a
modest leap of faith to conclude that concentrated wine
would have even greater healing power. Arnold of Villanova,
who taught at the medical school of Montpellier in France,
wrote around 1300 that *aqua vitae* was the water of immortality since it 'prolongs life, clears away ill-humors, revives the
heart, and maintains youth'.[2] *Aqua vitae* was called *brandewijn*
(burnt wine) by the Dutch and brandywine, or simply brandy,
by the English. One of the earliest centres for the production
of brandy was the city of Cognac. Brandy was one of the
first ardent spirits that seduced people away from low-alcohol
beverages such as beer and wine.

Curiously, the belief in the beneficial effects of brandy
would persist well into the twentieth century. Fanny Farmer,
principal of the Boston Cooking School and author of a

The Largest Still in Captivity, 1922. This photograph shows policemen and customs officers with the largest still to be confiscated in Washington, DC.

manual for nurses and caregivers published in 1905, considered brandy the most beneficial of the alcoholic beverages. She recommended an alcoholic drink if the patient had a weak pulse, a persistent high temperature, nervous exhaustion, tremor or low delirium, and in cases of shock or accident. She unabashedly recommended that 'eighteen to twenty ounces of brandy' could be 'administered daily without producing any intoxicating effects'. What was she drinking?

In time it was discovered that wine could be prevented from oxidizing and turning into vinegar by adding brandy. By controlling the kind of grapes used, the length of fermentation and a host of other variables, vintners in Spain and Portugal created sherry and port. These products are called fortified wines because of the higher alcoholic content contributed by the brandy. Eventually grapes grown on the island of Madeira off the coast of North Africa were made into a fortified wine called Madeira. All three were favourite after-dinner drinks and were dispensed at inns and taverns throughout England, North America and the Caribbean. Fortified wines gave people a taste for drinks with a higher level of alcohol and a greater buzz than they could get from beer or wine.

Over time it was learned that potatoes, malt and other starches could be converted into gin, sugar cane and molasses into rum and corn (Zea maize), rye and barley into whisky. The supply of pure alcohol continued to increase until it could be purchased by people with little means. A cheap and reliable supply of high-proof alcohol was the necessary next step for the creation of a cocktail. But we mustn't get ahead of our story here.

Before you can make a Martini you have to have gin, the first alcoholic distillate produced in quantity and available to the masses. Gin was flavoured with juniper berries (*Juniperus communis*) to mask the bad taste of cheaply made spirits. Gin, though also called geneva, did not originate in Switzerland. The name geneva comes from the French 'genèvre', meaning juniper berry. The development of gin is credited to Franz de le Boë (1614–1672), a professor of medicine at the University of Leyden in Holland, better known by his Latin name, Sylvius. Meant to be used only as medicine and dispensed by apothecaries, the drink soon spread to England where it was called Royal Poverty, because when beggars got high on gin, they imagined they were kings.[3]

England experienced a 'gin epidemic' between 1720 and 1751, when drinking cheap gin was the fashion among the poor. Alcohol consumption increased from 2 million gallons annually to about 11 million during this period.[4] Engraver William Hogarth captured this time of alcoholic excess in his work *Gin Lane* (1751), which depicts a syphilitic and stupefied woman who lets her child fall out of her arms as she reaches for her snuff.

In Jonathan Swift's satirical novel *Gulliver's Travels*, published at the beginning of the gin epidemic, he observed that English people, fictionalized as the primitives Yahoos, imported from foreign countries a 'Sort of Liquid' (spirits). This made them 'merry' by putting them out of their senses and:

> diverted all melancholy Thoughts, begat wild extravagant Imaginations in the Brain, raised our Hopes, and banished our Fears; suspended every Office of Reason for a Time, and deprived us of the Use of our Limbs, until we fell into a profound sleep; although it must be confessed, that we always awaked sick and dispirited; and that the Use of this Liquor filled us with Diseases, which made our Lives uncomfortable and short.[5]

Besides brandy, gin and fortified wine, it would be rum that facilitated increased alcohol consumption in Europe and the Americas. With the discovery of the New World by Christopher Columbus, the Caribbean was identified as fertile ground for the production of sugar. To meet production goals, the Portuguese imported slaves from Africa. Over time about 11 million slaves were brutally stolen from their homeland to work the sugar plantations in the Caribbean.

In Barbados it was discovered that a 'brandy' could be made cheaply from molasses, the then worthless byproduct of sugar making. At first this fiery drink was called 'killdevil' but it was later referred to as 'Rumbullion', a slang word with roots in southern England, where it meant a brawl, a not unlikely consequence of excess consumption. 'Rumbullion' was shortened over time to simply 'rum'.

After the American Revolution there was a surplus of sugar cane in the Caribbean and an excess of corn (Zea maize) in the USA. Because these agricultural products could easily be converted into alcohol, the quantity of rum and corn whiskey available skyrocketed and their prices plummeted. The unintended consequence was a greater demand for this cheap alcohol followed by overconsumption. It was in this alcoholic fog of drunken excess that the cocktail was born in America.

Cocktail: What's In a Name?

The word 'cocktail' first appeared in England to describe a horse that has had its tail docked to distinguish it as being of mixed breed. The term was also used to refer to a person who has assumed the position of a gentleman but lacks good breeding. It has been suggested that the idea of mixing a pure spirit with other ingredients, a mixed breed if you would, begged to be called a 'cock tail' or 'cocktail'.

The first citation for cocktail as a beverage in the *Oxford English Dictionary* is from the *Farmer's Cabinet* dated 28 April 1803: 'Drank a glass of cocktail – excellent for the head'. Another reference is found in the 13 May 1806 edition of the *Balance and Columbian Repository*, a newspaper published in Hudson, New York. A reader wrote to the editor inquiring about the use of the word 'cocktail' in an earlier edition of that paper. He wrote:

> Sir ... be so obliging as to inform me what is meant by this species of refreshment? ... never in my life ... did I hear of cocktail before ... does it signify that the Democrats who make the potion are turned topsy turvy, and have their heads where their tails are?

The editor responded:

Inn sign at The Bell in Hand Tavern, Boston, one of several taverns that claim to be America's oldest.

Cocktail is a stimulating liquor, composed of spirits of any kind, sugar, water, and bitters – it is vulgarly called a bitter sling and is supposed to be an excellent electioneering potion, inasmuch as it renders the heart stout and bold, at the same time that it fuddles the head. It is said also, to be of great use to a Democratic candidate: because, as person having swallowed a glass of it, is ready to swallow anything else.[6]

Because of this published description of the cocktail, 1806 is generally recognized as the birthday of this American invention. Many beverage-related associations and groups celebrated the bicentenary of the cocktail in 2006.

The Demon Liquor, *c.* 1870, oil on canvas. Who is the demon in this Temperance genre painting, the devil coming through the back door or the politician buying drinks and votes?

Another clue to its origins at the beginning of the nineteenth century can be found in 1809 in the writings of Washington Irving: 'those recondite beverages, cock-tail, stone-fence, and sherry cobbler'.[7]

Further evidence that the word has roots in New York State can be found in James Fenimore Cooper's *The Spy*, published in 1821. He describes a hotel keeper by the name of Betty as 'being the inventor of that beverage which is so well-known at the present hour . . . by the name "cocktail"'.[8] This novel, staged in the 1780s, is of course a work of fiction and cannot be used to date this beverage, but it does suggest that the word may have been in wide use and that Cooper felt confident in attributing the origin of the cocktail to the last quarter of the eighteenth century.

HAVE A COCKTAIL
WITH ME ?

Cocktails have always been associated with sex, as in this American postcard of *c.* 1900. When few women drank spirits, cocktails were frequently associated with loose women, prostitutes and entertainers.

Food historian Jeri Quinzio has identified other stories about the origin of the name 'cocktail'. One of these theories speculates that since cocktails originated in taverns the name might refer to the 'cock' or tap on a barrel. Since the dregs from the tap were called its tail or tailings, it is suggested that 'cocktail' evolved as a name for the last dregs from a tavern tap. Another theory is that since the consumption of alcoholic beverages, including cocktails, frequently occurred at breakfast, the drink might have been named after the cock's wakeup call.[9]

The word may have originated in a drinking bout in a New York tavern when patrons under the influence tried to outshine one another in naming some new concoction of alcohol, sugar and bitters. The use of compound words to describe alcoholic beverages had a long tradition in America. Every tippler and bartender had the opportunity to add a new word to the dictionary and gain fame and immortality.

By the time 'cocktail' came into common use other whimsical names, such as 'phlegm cutter', 'fog-driver', 'fillip', 'spur in the head' and 'stone-fence', were also popular. What is unique about the word 'cocktail' is that it did not stick as the name for just one beverage but for a whole class of potent drinks.

The solution to this name problem may have been staring scholars in the face for centuries. Samuel Johnson did not have an entry for cocktail in his dictionary of 1755 but he did include cóctile, a word that means baked or burnt, as in the baking of bricks.[10] At this time, in colonial America, it was a common practice to plunge a hot poker into a drink to warm it and change its taste. Could a New York chimney mason have used the word in a tavern to describe a newly made drink? The number of theories and explanations for the origin of cocktails is too long to be listed here. The true origin of the word is probably lost forever.

As a class, cocktails are the most American of alcoholic drinks and at the same time are the most international of beverages. Born in America after its independence, the cocktail was quickly transported to all corners of the globe. As Felten rightly points out in *How's Your Drink?*, cocktails were not a class of drinks at first but specific drinks such as the whiskey cocktail. Spirits, sugar, water and bitters made it a cocktail but the name depended on the spirits used. By the end of the nineteenth century 'cocktail' generally meant a mixed drink with bitters. By the time of the First World War it was more often a mixed drink served before dinner. Since Prohibition any mixed drink with or without bitters is a cocktail.

At its very essence a cocktail is a mixture of one or more alcoholic beverages, usually whisky, gin, vodka or tequila, with bitters or flavours added. It is usually served with an accent such as a lemon twist, olive, pearl onion, a slice of orange or, in the case of a Margarita, salt on the rim of the

A professional bartender knows his customers as well as he knows his drinks. Barry Carlin, head bartender at the 1640 Hart House Tavern in Ipswich, Massachusetts, the oldest building in America with an operating tavern.

glass. Cocktails are considered by some as a beverage to imbibe before dinner; others consider them the perfect postprandial indulgence. Regardless of what a cocktail is composed of, or when it is consumed, it is always served chilled; in fact, the colder the better. *Cabaret*, a salacious magazine that reported on America's night club scene in the 1950s, noted that cocktails in France and Italy were decadent, lacking in character and appalling because they were both weak and 'insufficiently iced'.[11]

Dale DeGroff, writing in the *Oxford Encyclopedia of Food and Drink in America*, observed that: 'Cocktails are shaken or stirred, rolled or muddled; they are dry or sweet, creamy or frozen. They are perfect or dirty; they are up or over. But one thing they are not is weak.' Whether it is in a hotel bar in New York City, Rome, Beijing, Tokyo or Rio de Janeiro, or on a cruise ship in the Caribbean, you can depend on finding a cocktail to suit your taste that is both strong and very cold.

Curiously, at the same time that the word 'cocktail' was coming into the vernacular, soda waters were being introduced to thirsty Americans. The first soda establishments in the USA were modelled after European spas and pump rooms. Ice cream historian Jeri Quinzio documents that a 'soda water concern' dispensing a variety of soda waters opened in New Haven, Connecticut, and at the Tontine Coffee House in New York City in 1807.[12] Druggists and chemists who dispensed these early waters, made with bicarbonate of soda, faced the same challenge as bartenders: what to call their creations. Some of these beverages went by the name of carbonade, mephitic julep, mephitic gas, seltzer, spa, gaseous alkaline, oxygenated waters or marble waters. In the end only seltzer, soda water and pop had any staying power.

Soda water compounded with flavouring took on a host of names suggestive of its more muscular cousin, the alcoholic cocktail, and some did contain small amounts of alcohol. The Sherry Cobbler was fashionable with women and was made with sherry, sugar, lemon and ice decorated with a fruit slice. The Siberian Flip was made with pineapple and orange juice with a touch of angostura bitters; Ambrosia with raspberry, vanilla and hock. Later on in the century ice cream was added to the menu at soda fountains, which – with a nod to the evolving cocktail culture – were sometimes called 'ice cream saloons'.

2

Punch, the Cocktail's Original Ancestor

Before the cocktail there was punch, drawn from a British obsession with deep roots in India. It was in the British colonies, in both the Caribbean and North America, that the art of formulating a punch was perfected. Punch is important to our story because it was the prototype for all cocktails.

In 1757 the son of Boston's stern Puritan leader, Cotton Mather, sent a box of lemons to a friend with these lines:

> You know from Eastern India came
> The skill of making punch as did the name.
> And as the name consists of letters five,
> By five ingredients is it kept alive.

Most references claim that the word 'punch' derives from the Hindustani word *panch*, meaning five, referring to the five ingredients originally used in the drink: arrack (spirits distilled from palm sugar), sugar, lemons, water or tea and a spice. The ingredients were also referred to as the 'strong' (alcohol), the 'lights' (water, tea or white wine), the 'sour' (citrus), the 'sweet' (sugar) and the 'spice' (nutmeg). This so-called 'Rule of Five' was also expressed as 'One sour; Two sweet; Three strong, Four weak, and spices make Five.'

Arrack, the original spirit used for making punch, was produced from the action of wild yeast on palm sugar extracted from the cut flowers of the coconut palm (*Cocos nucifera*). The watery sap, called 'toddy', was allowed to ferment and then distilled into a spirit. The name comes from the Arabic word *araq*, meaning 'sweat' or 'strong liquor', and is reported to have the taste and smell of rum. In the Philippines the distillate is called Lambanog. In colonial America a toddy was a popular tavern drink composed of rum, water and sugar, dusted with nutmeg.

Outside Asia bartenders turned to rum to make their punches because of the limited supply of arrack. Casanova, the eighteenth-century Italian who documented his sexual conquests in his literary work *The Story of My Life*, also commented

Making punch has always been a male prerogative. Margaret Dovaston (1884–1954), *Good Cheer*.

— Make haste with the Sangaree, Quashie and tell Quaco to drive the Birds up to me — I'm ready.

A West India Sportsman, 1807, hand-coloured aquatint. The caption reads: 'Make haste with the Sangaree, Quashie, and tell Quaco to drive the Birds up to me – I'm ready.'

on his food and drink cravings. He wrote that arrack was losing its popularity as an ingredient in making punch and rum was being substituted for it. In America it was Jamaican rum that was the preferred ingredient.

Benjamin Franklin, one of America's leading statesmen and signatory of the Declaration of Independence, celebrated punch in 1737 in his publication *Poor Richard's Almanack* with the following poem:

> Boy, bring a Bowl of China here,
> Fill it with Water cool and clear:
> Decanter with Jamaica right,
> And Spoon of Silver clean and bright,
> Sugar twice-fin'd, in pieces cut,
> Knife, Sieve and Glass, in order put,
> Bring forth the fragrant Fruit, and then
> We're happy till the Clock Strikes Ten.

Punch making took time, planning, the right ingredients, concentration and appreciative friends.

A new theory, put forward in the *Oxford Encyclopedia of Food and Drink in America*, argues that the name 'punch' came from sailors' talk for a puncheon, the type of cask used for transporting rum. Lending credibility to this idea are the many words, some drink-related, which seamen contributed

Russian sailors gather on deck to take their grog break in 1893.

to the English language. 'Grog' is one that had staying power. Grog was a sailor's daily ration of rum diluted with water. Aboard ship it was ladled out of a butt, the name of a large barrel used for transporting wine. When sailors gathered around the scuttled (full of water) butt, to take their allowance of grog, they would pass on gossip, hence the origin of the word 'scuttlebutt'.[1]

Supposedly, grog was invented by British Vice-Admiral Edward Vernon, who had command of a squadron of five ships in the West Indies during the 1740s. Admiral Vernon is remembered less for his military conquests, including the capture of Guantánamo from the Spanish in 1741, than for the order he gave in 1740 requiring the diluting of a sailors' rum ration with water. His sailors called the drink 'grog', reportedly because his men called Admiral Vernon 'Old Grog' for the grogram (a coarse and stiff fabric made of silk and mohair) coat he wore. But this story may have to be scuttled

George Cruikshank, *The Sailor's Description of a Chase and Capture*, 1822, hand-coloured etching. A group of sailors hang on an old salt's every word while imbibing plenty of grog.

because the English author Daniel Defoe had one of his characters use the word 'grog' in reference to rum from Barbados in his book *The Family Instructor* (1718).[2]

The mixing of water with a liquor other than rum and calling it 'grog' had a tradition in colonial Virginia, where George Washington had his estate.[3] It cannot go unsaid that Lawrence Washington, George's older half-brother, served on Vernon's flagship, *Princess Caroline*, as a Captain of the Marines in 1741 and named his estate Mount Vernon in honour of his commander. George Washington inherited the property upon the death of Lawrence's widow in 1761.

The English gentry took very quickly to punch and developed social customs as to how, when and where it was to be made. An essential part of punch making was the bowl itself, often made of porcelain and imported from China. These colourful and exotic-looking bowls added to the allure of this beverage with Eastern origins. The British even invented a punchbowl known as a Monteith, named for a Scot called 'Monsieur Monteith', a man of fashion who wore a cloak with a scalloped edge. The rim of this bowl was crenulated like its namesake's coat, forming indentations from which a ladle, lemon strainer and tall wine-glasses were hung.[4]

Punch became popular in the New World just as it did in old England. People of means purchased punch bowls from merchants trading with China. It might have taken a year or more for a specially ordered bowl to arrive. Every dinner was prefaced by a bowl of punch. Double and 'thribble'

George Cruikshank, *Economy*, hand-coloured etching, 1816.
Politician Henry Peter Brougham famously criticized the extravagance and favouritism of the court. Here, in the guise of John Bull, he appears to the Prince Regent (later George IV), who is drinking a large bowl of punch.

bowls were served in taverns; these held two and three quarts (1.9 or 2.8 litres) each.

Drinking punch in a colonial tavern was a convivial affair, shared at a common table with friends, neighbours and acquaintances and cutting across social lines. Sometimes it was served from smaller bowls that were passed around from person to person, with each taking a sip before passing it on. At the ordination of the Revd Joseph McKean in 1785 in Massachusetts, the tavern keeper left the following bill for 80 people who attended a morning meal and 68 who came to dinner:

> 30 bowles of Punch before the People went to meeting
> 44 bowles of punch while at dinner, besides
> 28 bottles of wine and 8 bowls of Brandy
> Same amount of Cherry Rum, and 6 people drank tea.[5]

To be fair, the punchbowl was probably small, holding about a cup of liquid.

Punch making was a male prerogative and a serious business whether in the home or at a tavern. As depicted in period paintings and lithographs, the punch maker would line up his ingredients and paraphernalia ahead of time to be certain he had everything. On the table before him would be a basket of lemons, limes or oranges, a pitcher of water, a cone of rock-hard loaf-sugar from the Caribbean, wrapped in blue indigo paper, sugar snips, a sharp knife for cutting the skin off citrus fruit, a ladle, a pot of brewed tea if it was being used as the 'light', a nutmeg grater and a nutmeg. Spirits – rum, brandy, gin or whisky – would be displayed in their green corked bottles. Assembling the punch was done with dramatic flair and often accompanied by a running commentary from the host.

The juices of lemons, oranges, limes, guava and pineapples harvested in the Caribbean and imported to New England were all used in punches. A Boston fruit importer operating under the name Basket of Lemmons placed the following advertisement in the *Salem Gazette* of 1741:

> Extraordinary good and very fresh Orange juice which some of the very best Punch Tasters prefer to Lemmon, at one dollar a gallon. Also very good Lime Juice and Shrub to put into Punch at the Basket of Lemmons, J. Crosby, Lemmon Trader.

The final action was for the host to remove the citrus peel in one continuous curlicue and drape it over the edge of the punch bowl to signify that it was freshly made. Countless Dutch still-life paintings of the period depict punchbowls with the signature lemon curlicue. This peel may explain why a lemon twist, a slice of orange or wedges of lime are popular cocktail garnishes today. Their presence was a signal to the customer that their drink was freshly made.

A New England landlord left to posterity the following instructions for making a proper punch:

> The man who sees, does, or thinks of anything else while he is making Punch may as well look for the Northwest Passage on Mutton Hill. A man can never make good punch unless he is satisfied, nay positive, that no man breathing can make better. I can and do make good Punch, because I do nothing else, and this is my way of doing it. I retire to a solitary corner with my ingredients ready sorted; they are as follows, and I mix them in the order they are here written. Sugar, twelve tolerable lumps; hot water, one pint; lemons, two, the juice and peel; old

Garnishes. Fresh fruit from the Caribbean and olives from the Mediterranean attest to the global influence of the cocktail.

Jamaica rum, two gills; brandy, one gill; porter or stout, half a gill; arrack, a slight dash. I allow myself five minutes to make a bowl in the foregoing proportions, carefully stirring the mixture as I furnish the ingredients until it actually foams; and then Kangaroos! how beautiful it is![6]

Punches were named for people and places; taverns and hosts; bartenders and stage-coach drivers; unusual ingredients and romantic incidents. The following recipe for 'Connecticut Colonial Punch' is an example, naming a punch after one of the thirteen original colonies:

Of oranges four and lemons two
You take the juice to make your brew;
Eight tablespoons of sugar fine,
A quart of good red Bordeaux wine,
A large spoonful of choice Jamaica
Will give a flavor delicious later.
Then a generous wine glass of old Cognac
Will make your lips begin to smack,

But wait until you add the sparkling champagne
A pint at least or your labor's in vain.[7]

Besides punch there were many compounded drinks
made in American taverns and inns that were served in individual cups or mugs. These were made mostly with rum and
a mixture of one or more of the following ingredients:
molasses, butter, milk, whipped cream, beaten egg whites,
spices (cinnamon, nutmeg, mace) sugar syrup, ale or cider. A
toddy was rum mixed with sugar and water; sangre, a mixture
of wine or beer sweetened with sugar and flavoured with
nutmeg; flip, strong beer with rum and sugar or molasses, or
even dried pumpkin. These drinks were served at room temperature, heated at the hearth or, in the case of flip, baptized
with a 'loggerhead' or hot poker. Except for spiked eggnog
during the Christmas and New Year holidays or hot toddies
at a ski lodge, traditional colonial-style drinks have almost
disappeared from the American drink repertoire.

As noted in chapter One, by 1806 cocktails, as a distinctive American beverage, were taking hold, at least in New
York State. In February of that same year an event was play-
ing out in Boston that would change the cocktail forever and
ensure it future global success. That winter, Frederic Tudor
harvested a load of ice from a local pond and shipped it to
the West Indian island of Martinique. Bostonians laughed up
their sleeves at Tudor's foolhardy and 'slippery speculation'.[8]
The next year he shipped a cargo of ice to Cuba; in 1810, to
Jamaica; in 1833, 200 tons of ice to Calcutta; and the next
year he sent a cargo to Rio de Janeiro.

For thousands of years ice had been harvested in the
cold months and stored in underground caverns or silos.
But its use was restricted only to the rich and powerful. It was
Tudor's vision that if ice could be reduced in price, everyone,

including those with limited resources, would want it. Furthermore, he was convinced that they would welcome cold drinks and other iced refreshments such as ice cream.

When barmen were introduced to ice for the first time, they used it in wasteful ways and then doubled the price of the cold drink over the cost of a warm one. As a result customers went to another bar. To develop a market for iced bar drinks, Tudor promoted the idea of giving an influential barkeeper free ice for a year on condition that he sold his liquors cold without an increase in price. It was his belief that other bartenders would follow the practice or lose their customers.

The *Illustrated London News* in 1845 commented on the purity of ice from America, noting that it was the custom there 'to mix it with water or milk, for drinking; to dilute it with wines or spirits'. The same article observed that some of London's 'hotels and taverns are beginning to use this ice for the manufacture of "Mint-juleps", "Sherry-cobblers", and

Ice harvesting was a big business in mid-19th-century America. This location at Spy Pond in West Cambridge, Massachusetts, employed hundreds and yielded 6,000 tons of ice a day during the winter season.

Martini cocktail in the iconic Martini glass.

other American beverages of celebrity; and we should not be surprised, if these tempting drinks, as well as the ice itself, were to come into very general use.'[9] *The European Times* that same year was already reporting that ice had 'become an essential element in the civic fetes' at the London Coffee House, the London Tavern, Long's Hotel and 'at every establishment of a similar kind of any celebrity in London'.[10] Clearly, the use of ice in drinks on both sides of the Atlantic was hot news.

With the advent of the cocktail, pewter cups, wooden noggins, punch bowls and ceramic mugs slowly disappeared from the bar. The word 'cocktail', which may have started out as the whimsical name for a particular combination of alcohol and other ingredients, took on a new meaning: that of a class of mixed alcoholic beverages, each with their own distinctive name and specifically shaped glass.

3

American Taverns,
the Cocktail's Nursery

America's taverns, saloons and hotel bars provided the perfect nursery in which the cocktail could mature into manhood during the nineteenth century. For the next hundred years it remained almost exclusively a man's drink. The cocktail evolved as a nocturnal drink, something a man could imbibe at the end of a long day. It was used for unwinding. Served in an individual glass, it could be consumed anonymously at a hotel bar or in the company of friends or business associates. For most of the nineteenth century the cocktail was still too undomesticated and too masculine to be consumed at home, where women drank tea, sipped sherry or took a medicinal brandy for their health.

One common element in taverns, saloons, pubs, taprooms and cocktail lounges is the bar. In the colonial tavern the bar was not a counter, longer than it was wide, over which drinks were served. Rather, it was a small room, called a cage bar, generally located in one corner of the main room. When not in use, wooden bars or slats, which extended from the counter-top to the ceiling, were locked in place. The bar was open when the tavern-keeper entered the cage bar through a door from his private quarters and raised the bars, signalling to his guests that he was ready to mix drinks. This protective

George Cruikshank, *The Modern Punch-maker*, 1806, hand-coloured etching.

bar was necessary in order to protect the innkeeper's valuable inventory of imported ceramic punch bowls from China, imported distilled spirits such as Dutch gin and French brandy, demijohns filled with fortified wine from Madeira, cane sugar and ripe citrus fruit from the Caribbean and nutmeg from the Spice Islands.

Everything that came in contact with the bar picked up the prefix of 'bar'. The woman who carried the drinks to your table was the barmaid; spills were wiped up with a bar mop. The first documented use of the word 'bartender', to designate the man who mixed the drinks came in 1836.[1] Nathaniel Hawthorne marvelled at the barman's flashy dexterity in his novel *The Blithedale Romance* (1852):

> With a tumbler in each hand he tossed the contents from one to the other. Never conveying it awry, nor spilling the least drop, he compelled the frothy liquor, as it seemed

to me, to spout forth from one glass and descend into the other, in a great parabolic curve, as well-defined and calculable as a planet's orbit.[2]

The importance of taverns and inns as watering holes in which men could socialize diminished with the advent of the railroad and the decline of the stagecoach. Men of means increasingly turned to saloons and cafes as they grew in popularity, and working-class men turned to neighbourhood bars or taprooms for their needs. Besides alcohol, many of these establishments provided a free lunch, as well as being places where patrons could learn about job openings and where labour unions could recruit members. Men went to the local bar to play pool or cards, buy pornography or drugs, or find a prostitute. But for most blue-collar workers a bar was a place to get a beer or whiskey – or both (called a 'shot and a beer') – in an attempt to 'tie one on'. Saloon-goers

An original cage bar was used to protect valuable liquors, punch bowls and paraphernalia. The Old Tavern, Eastfield Village, New York.

expected to be transported beyond the boring confines of their daily life or the misery of their factory jobs. They wanted, as historian Madelon Powers found, to experience the 'joys of intoxication and euphoria'.[3] This experience was described with colourful and playful language as being fuzzled, flushed, cockeyed, bamboozled, balmy, bent and woozy.

The wall behind these neighbourhood bars was adorned with shelves of liquor bottles, but they were mostly for show. As one writer put it, workingmen's saloons were not 'the happy hunting grounds for cocktails, cobblers, fizzes and sours'.[4] You had to travel uptown, out of working-class neighbourhoods, if you wanted a cocktail.

The popularity of cross-country railroad travel created a demand for hotels, which in turn created a need for hotel bars modelled after big city saloons. Since hotels catered to an upscale population with more disposable income and leisure time, they invested heavily in original works of art, marble, maple and mirrors in order to create a rich and inviting drinking environment. As people on both sides of the Atlantic travelled for both business and pleasure, resort hotels and steamship companies added bars and lounges to meet consumers' needs. All of these institutions promoted the consumption of cocktails, and made it socially acceptable. One of the most popular hotel bars in New York City in the last half of the nineteenth century was the palatial Hoffman House. William F. Mulhall wrote an account of his experience as one of seventeen men behind the bar. He was the youngest, just past twenty. He described the bar as 'a magnificent structure of carved mahogany, the mirrors that lined the walls were said to be the largest in America . . . and every detail of the furniture and fixtures was of the most elegant and costly kind'. Behind the bar hung *Nymphs and Satyr* by the French artist William-Adolphe Bouguereau, portraying a group of nymphs bathing in a woodland pond surprised by a satyr. This evocative painting was surrounded with other paintings 'crowded with nude figures'. Bouguereau's painting was discovered in storage in the 1930s and now hangs in the Sterling and Francine Clark Art Institute in Williamstown, Massachusetts.

Mulhall wrote that the Hoffman was the 'most palatial drinking-room in the entire world'. One day a week was 'Ladies' Day'. But a woman could not just walk in unaccompanied. Ladies were escorted through the bar because the bar and its environment were 'a resort for gentlemen'.[5]

The opulence that some bar owners tried to create was not always appreciated. T. S. Arthur, the author of *Ten Nights in a Bar-room* (1855), a novel promoting Temperance, tried to bring attention to the degrading influence of demon liquor. The action in the book takes place at the Sickle and Sheaf, a rural American tavern. He described the bar as having 'a polished brass rod or railing' that

> embellished the counter, and sundry ornamental attractions had been given to the shelving behind the bar – such as mirrors, gilding, etc. Pictures, too, were hung upon the walls, or more accurately speaking, coarse coloured lithographs, the subjects of which, if not really obscene, were flashing, or vulgar.[6]

The cocktails that the public called for at the Hoffman were the Old Fashioned, the whiskey cocktail, the absinthe cocktail, the Turf-club, the Martini and the Bronx cocktail. Prohibition marked the end of New York City's great hotel bars.

Anyone who has ever lingered at a bar and watched a skilled bartender perform his magic has a sense that more is taking place than just the mixing of alcohol, sugars and

Interior view of the Hoffman House bar, 1890, print.

botanicals into a glass with ice. Some have likened the making of a cocktail to art, even theatre, with the bar as the stage and the bartender as performer. Salvatore Calabrese in his book *Classic Cocktails* finds that the bartender 'is doctor, psychologist and psychiatrist in one'.[7] Joseph Lanza, writing in *Esquire* magazine, argues that the making and consumption of cocktails has all the elements of a religious ceremony. 'The bartender is the high priest, the drink is the sacramental cup, and the cocktail lounge is . . . a temple or cathedral.'[8] But like other religions, the cult of the cocktail has its purists and its heretics. The orthodox worshipper of the Martini doesn't want to see anything in his glass but gin, vermouth – at a 30 to 1 ratio, of course – and an olive. To add Cointreau or anything else into the mix is blasphemy.

Over the past 200 years tens of thousands of concoctions have been formulated by bartenders, mixologists and amateurs. Like colourful and dazzling fireworks, they flash across the alcoholic horizon and burst upon the scene, but most soon fizzle out. Only a small number of drinks have had the rocket power to go into orbit to join the galaxy of classic cocktails. Still, cocktail experts, like globe-trotting writer Naren Young, believe that we are witnessing a 'global cocktail renaissance'.[9] The classics are being rediscovered and given a contemporary twist. New spirits, at least to those outside their place of origin, are emerging from South America and Asia and have the potential to spawn a new generation of classic cocktails.

American postcard, *c.* 1948.

A Manhattan cocktail.

Every cocktail has a story to tell. In fact, some have too many stories associated with them for us to be certain when or by whom they were created. Trying to identify the original ingredients that went into a concoction can be a tedious if not hopeless pursuit. For example, there is the claim that the Manhattan was first formulated with whiskey, syrup and bitters by a Maryland bartender in 1846 to revive a wounded duellist. When vermouth was substituted for syrup in New York City, it took its present name.[10] Another source traces the drink to Winston Churchill's American mother, Jennie, who had it served at a banquet at New York's Manhattan Club.[11]

A Margarita. This drink has evolved, like the Martini, into a separate class of cocktails.

The Margarita, like the Martini, is now viewed as a classic whether shaken or frozen, or infused with watermelon or prickly pear. It has served as an inspiration to a new generation of mixologists. In testimony to the global reach of the Margarita, John Burdett uses the drink – perfect with viscous ice, salt glittering around the rim of wide glasses and generous shots of tequila – in his provocative mystery novel *Bangkok 8* to set the mood in the Bamboo Bar at the Oriental Hotel in Bangkok, Thailand.[12]

In 1971 Mariano Martinez, owner of a Tex-Mex restaurant in Dallas, Texas, made a pitcher of frozen Margaritas in a soft-serve ice cream machine, creating a frozen slushy with the kick of a donkey. The frozen Margarita was an instant success and resulted in tequila sales in the USA increasing 1,500 per cent between 1975 and 1995. The original machine is now in the Smithsonian Museum in Washington, DC.[13]

There are even more conflicting claims about the origin of the Margarita, the tequila cocktail made with triple sec or Cointreau and lime juice. By one account it was created in the 1930s at a race track in Tijuana, Mexico. Another has its place of origin at the Garci Crespo Hotel in Puebla, Mexico. Yet another story has it being invented at The Tale of the Cock Restaurant in Los Angeles in the 1950s.[14] Regardless of who invented this drink, it was college students in the 1960s who put tequila on the map and the Margarita on the bar.

In 1856 Andrew Heublein came to Hartford, Connecticut, from Suhl, Bavaria, with his two sons, Gilbert and Louis. This small producer and importer of alcohol might have folded during America's Prohibition era but for its one profitable product, a condiment for meat known as A1 sauce.[15] After running a distinguished restaurant they launched a bottled cocktail business under the name of G. F. Heublein & Bro. The company is now a branch of the global beverage giant Diageo.

The creation of bottled cocktails, called The Club, was the result of a rained-out picnic. The Heublein Café prepared a gallon of Martinis and a gallon of Manhattans for the big day. Normally the pre-mixed drinks would have been thrown out but a helper reportedly tasted the cocktails and said they were pretty good. The idea to market pre-mixed cocktails to area clubs was born, hence the name The Club. The product has been a success since 1892.[16]

Heublein had two stunning successes in the twentieth century that put the company in the cocktail hall of fame. Besides inventing the bottled cocktail, Heublein was the first company to see a future for vodka, a fiery spirit that was little known in America and considered a crude beverage.

In the 1860s Piotr Arsenievich Smirnov established the Smirnov vodka distillery in Russia. His son Vladimir Smirnov took over the company in 1910 but lost it during the Russian Revolution when the Bolsheviks shut it down. Vladimir was imprisoned and sentenced to death but escaped. In 1924 he moved the company to Lwów (formerly Poland, now Lviv, Ukraine) and changed the name from Smirnov to Smirnoff, the French spelling of the family name.

In the 1930s a distant relative of the Heubleins, Cambridge-educated John Gilbert Martin, became vice president of the company. He brought with him an uncanny ability to look into the future and a bit of luck. He learned that Rudolph Kunett of Bethel, Connecticut, only 50 miles away from Heublein, had acquired the patent to make Smirnoff. Heublein purchased the rights to the Smirnoff name in 1939. Because of the Second World War, marketing was put on hold until 1946. Vodka was a weak seller until Jack Morgan, the owner of the Cock 'n Bull Restaurant in Los Angeles, and his friend John Martin of Heublein concocted a drink of vodka, lime juice and ginger beer and called it the Moscow Mule.[17] This cocktail introduced vodka to the world as a cocktail mixer.

One of the most unusual cocktails ever created in the nineteenth century was called the Brompton, probably a reference to London's Brompton Hospital. This cocktail consisted of gin, honey and morphine and was often given to the terminally ill. In fact, it was sometimes called the Terminal cocktail.[18] The names for alcoholic beverages are as colourful as names given to horses in the Kentucky Derby. In fact, the Crown Royal Canadian Whisky Company created the Crown of Roses and the Royal Stretch to celebrate the sport of horseracing.

Most drinkers today recognize the name Martini as designating a class of drinks made from gin or vodka which fall into the family of cocktails. 'Cocktails' was not always the overarching designation for compounded alcoholic drinks. Until the 1950s drinks were listed both in books and on menus under a very broad category called 'mixed drinks'. A lunch menu aboard the ss *Ambassador* in 1936 sorted mixed drinks into highballs, cocktails, fizzes, rickeys, whiskies, cordials, flips and sours and grouped Collins, punches and cobblers under a separate catch-all category. At the bottom of the menu all cobblers, daisies and smashes were priced at 40 cents each without naming them. A drink book called *300 Ways to Mix Drinks*, published in 1945, divided the drink index into cobblers, cocktails, Collins, coolers, fizzes, flips, highballs, mulled drinks, punches, rickeys, sangaries, shrubs, slings, smashes, sours, swizzles and toddies. On the menu and in books the Martini fell under the broad category of cocktails.

A highball, even if the word sounds a little old fashioned today, is universally recognized as a member of a class of cocktails composed of a base spirit and a generous portion of a non-alcoholic mixer such as soda water (seltzer), served in a tall glass with a simple garnish. Seven and Seven (7-UP), gin and tonic and rum and Coke are a few examples. One theory is that the name highball derived from the nineteenth-century practice of raising a ball on a pole to signal a train engineer to speed up.[19] Another is that it was a late afternoon drink, to be imbibed when the sun (ball) is high on the horizon.[20] Yet another speculates that the name crossed the Atlantic from Ireland, where a glass of whiskey was called 'a ball of fire'. When mixed with soda water and ice it became a highball.

The bad boy of cocktails is absinthe. Absinthe takes its name from the Latin for wormwood, *Artemisia absinthium*. At the beginning of the twentieth century, food adulteration crusader Harvey Wiley, former chief chemist of the US Department of Agriculture and head of the US Food and Drug Administration, had no kind words for this beverage. He said that the 'victims of absinth are more to be pitied . . . than those of alcohol, opium, or cocain'. He thought that it broke 'down the morale, sometimes paralyzing, or deranging digestion and general health, and reducing the victim to complete subjugation'. He claimed that the 'extremely revolting' symptoms of absinthe poisoning included delirium, hallucinations and paralysis.[21]

The high ball (today a green light) is still used in America to alert a train engineer that the track ahead is clear, as at The Conway Scenic Railroad, North Conway, New Hampshire..

Henri Privat-Livemont, *Absinthe Robette*, 1896, lithograph. Absinthe, once
the bad boy of spirits, is now back on the shelf and in duty free shops
around the globe.

In 1912 the US Department of Agriculture banned absinthe and all foods and drinks made with it. The French, thinking that the drink was undermining the character of its citizens during the hostilities in Europe, also banned it. By 1915 the sale of absinthe was banned in most of Europe except for Spain and the UK.

The US law on absinthe was updated in 1972 to ban only thujone, the active compound in wormwood in concentrations greater than 10 milligrams per kilogram. In 2007 absinthe became legally available in the USA and most other countries.[22]

The cocktail getting a bad name this century is the energy drink cocktail. It seems that mixing alcohol with so-called energy drinks is all the rage with college students who want to drink more, for longer. Energy drinks are carbonated beverages that contain large amounts of caffeine, sugar and vitamins. They are primarily marketed to people between the ages of eighteen and 30 as a stimulant, with the implied promise that they will improve a person's strength, power or sex drive. The active ingredient in these energy drinks is caffeine. Mary Claire O'Brien, MD, associate professor of emergency medicine at Wake Forest University School of Medicine, uses the analogy that mixing a stimulant (caffeine) with a depressant (alcohol) is like stepping on the accelerator and brakes of a car at the same time. In other words, O'Brien says, 'the symptoms of drunkenness are reduced, but not the drunkenness'.[23] Recipes using energy drinks as a base can be found on the Internet: the Electric Screwdriver, made with 2 ounces of vodka and 6 ounces each of orange juice and an energy drink, and the Quick and Easy, using an energy drink, with brandy and a blend of cranberry and raspberry juice, are only two examples.[24] Researchers have found that students who consume these cocktails are twice as likely to be hurt, injured or taken advantage of sexually than those who do not mix caffeine with alcohol. O'Brien reported at a meeting of the American Public Health Association that 29 states attorneys general have already publicly condemned alcoholic energy drinks.

4
The Globalization
of the Cocktail

I like to have a Martini
Two at the very most –
After three I'm under the table,
After four I'm under my host.
Dorothy Parker[1]

Towards the end of the nineteenth century and the beginning of the twentieth, the world witnessed the rapid spread of the cocktail outside the USA. The first American bar in London is reported to have been the Criterion, which opened in around 1910.[2]

American troops stationed in Europe during the First World War and an increase in the number of US students at European universities, along with business travel, brought American ideas and fashion, including the cocktail, to European shores. The large number of Americans and Europeans with disposable income and new ideas about how to use leisure time helped spread the cocktail's reputation.

The heyday of the international passenger liner during this period also helped in no small way to globalize the cocktail. It was in smoking rooms aboard steamships travelling between the USA, England and other European ports that non-Americans tasted their first cocktails. These smoking rooms would later evolve into lounges, bars or cabarets aboard modern-day cruise ships.

Smoking rooms were modelled after the finest hotel bars in America's largest cities. The smoking room aboard the Cunard liner *Aquitania* was described in 1914 as characteristic of the lounges found in the best men's clubs in London and New York.[3] Like the finest Manhattan bars, this room was panelled in walnut and richly ornamented with inlay and carving. Cunard's RMS *Tyrrhenia* was designed in an early Italian Renaissance style with stone plaster and panelling in Italian walnut. On the White Star Line's *Georgia* even the tourist smoking room was decorated in 'half timber and rough plaster, with an old tiled floor, antique furniture, casement windows in leaded glass' to capture the charm and friendliness of an old English farmhouse. Many of the rooms designed for first-class passengers contained a wood-burning fireplace. The Cunard Royal Mail steamer *Campania* boasted

Illustration from *The Savoy Cocktail Book* (1937), published by the Savoy Hotel in London – a sign that US cocktail culture had arrived in high society in Britain.

Postcard of
the observation
lounge and
cocktail bar
on the RMS
Mauretania,
built in 1906.

that its smoking room was designed as 'a fine baronial hall, with oaken walls, and seats of carved oak'. First-class passengers had access to the 'best of cigars and tobacco, an attentive barkeeper, and an unlimited cellar of the choicest liquids'.[4] These smoking rooms were designed to encourage the man of affairs to spend his days and evenings in pampered leisure.

Before there were cocktail menus, customers generally had to go to the bar to order a mixed drink. A 'Bill of Fare' dated 25 November 1895 from the steamship *Kansas City* instructed patrons to purchase their 'mixed liquors . . . at the bar', an indication that at this early date in steamship travel it was gentlemanly to order a bottle of brand-name liquor to be delivered to the table to be consumed neat or mixed with soda water (seltzer). In a short time cocktail menus appeared aboard ship, some with an extensive list of choices. The *Americana* and *Westchester* owned by the Meseck Steamboat Corporation listed thirteen cocktails on their 1936 menu card: the American Cocktail, Manhattan, Bronx, Dry Martini, Orange Blossom, Alexander, Bacardi, Jack Rose, Old Fashioned, Stinger, Side Car, Daiquiri and Cuba Libre. In that same year the Colonial Line listed eleven cocktails including the Tom Collins, Pink Lady and Gin Rickey. On

Soldiers and airmen were fighting for more than country and the girl back home.

another Colonial Line steamer you could get a Ward 8, Gin Fizz or Gin Sour. A cocktail menu dated April 1936 from the bar of the ss *Ambassador* listed 69 named cocktails organized by category.

Americans, already familiar with cocktails, introduced their travelling companions from around the world to their first taste of an authentic American libation. After returning from the USA these travellers helped spread the merits of the new mixed drinks. Europe's hotels and cafes added cocktails to their offerings in order to cater to the expectations and drinking preferences of American tourists, and soon the rest of the world would follow. Some European bars were simply called the 'American Bar'. In Graham Greene's novel *Brighton Rock* (1938), a meeting takes place between Colleoni and 'the Boy', two opposing gang leaders, in the lounge at the Cosmopolitan hotel in Brighton. As they talked, 'chimes of laughter came from the American Bar and the chink, chink, chink of ice'.[5] When they talk again by phone, 'the Boy' hears 'a glass chink and ice move in a shaker'. Greene uses the sound of cocktails being made to demonstrate the wide cultural gulf between the young street thug and the older and supposedly more sophisticated mob leader who does his business at the fashionable American bar.

By the 1960s airline passengers could have cocktails served by shapely stewardesses in mini skirts. Some airline executives and customers viewed stewardesses as flying cocktail hostesses. As planes got bigger and more people had to be served in a limited amount of time, airlines embraced a more practical approach to beverage service with an emphasis on liquor served in tiny nips, small glass or plastic bottles containing about 1½ fluid oz (44 ml). Until 2005 South Carolina law required that bartenders

Postcard advertising Jack Dempsey's Broadway Restaurant in New York, owned by the world heavyweight boxing champion.

make cocktails with nips instead of free-pouring or measuring into a jigger.

Despite the availability of comfortable international aircraft such as the Boeing 707, the ss *France* was launched in May 1960. By this time the male-dominated smoking room was gone. Aboard the ss *France* the best elements found in smoking rooms, bars, lounges and cabarets of the past half century were combined to create the Café de Paris with the 'longest bar afloat'. The liquor inventory on each sailing included 1,300 bottles of whiskey, Scotch whisky, brandy, gin and rum; 1,100 bottles of liqueurs; 1,200 bottles of champagne; and 8,500 bottles of wine.[6]

The last quarter of the twentieth century saw the advent of the cruise ship not as a means of travel but a destination in itself. Some of these ships could be described as floating cocktail lounges. Besides cocktails at dinner and in the casinos, you could order a frozen Daiquiri at the piano bar, a gin and tonic at the sports bar, a Martini in the jazz club, a Manhattan at the cigar bar, a themed drink in the entertainment lounges, a Mojito at the pool bars or anything in the world with room service. In fact, aboard ship you are never more than a few feet away from a Cosmopolitan.

While it is true that some of the most popular cocktails had their origin in the USA it wasn't long before Europe and Asia began to contribute their own classic mixes to the list of world-class cocktails. Outside the USA one of the most important influences was the British Navy, whose tars had brought the taste of punch, the prototype of all cocktails, to the British Isles from India. They opened their on-board medicine chests to search for an antidote to modify the harsh taste of British gin. The best gins were flavoured with juniper berries, but some distillers in London flavoured it with turpentine when they recognized that the active ingredient in both was a class of chemicals called terpenes.

British sailors found two promising candidates: Angostura bitters and quinine. Angostura bitters is an aromatic compound made from herbs. It was created by Dr Johann Siegert, a German medical doctor who sought adventure and joined Simón Bolívar of Venezuela in his fight against Spain. Bolívar appointed him Surgeon-General of the Military Hospital in 1824 in the town of Angostura, Venezuela, today called Ciudad Bolívar. Angostura bitters are now produced in Port-of-Spain, Trinidad.[7] Siegert created his bitters as a treatment for fevers and stomach disorders and the Royal Navy carried them to treat fevers. When mixed with gin the resulting drink was pink, creating the cocktail called Pink Gin.

The Royal Navy is also credited with inventing the gin and tonic. Quinine, a medicinal tonic used for combating malaria, was also found in the Royal Navy's medicine cabinet. Sailors mixed this tonic with gin, probably to cut the bitter

Pink Gin cocktails and cocktail shaker.

The Tom Collins, also known by its many aliases: John in London, Peter in Australia and Mike in Ireland.

taste. With a squeeze of lime, also on board as a cure for scurvy (the reason British sailors were called Limeys), you have a gin and tonic.

Mixing bitter herbs, botanicals and even quinine with alcohol to create a therapeutic tonic was common practice in the nineteenth century. These infusions, tinctures, elixirs and restoratives, all heavily laced with pure spirits, ensured brisk sales. If it didn't cure you, at least you got a momentary kick.

When Europe's hotels added an American Bar a new generation of European bartenders brought their creative ideas to the bar. The Tom Collins is a case in point. The Tom Collins derived its name from John Collins, head waiter at Limmer's Hotel in London. He made his sour with Old Tom gin, lemon juice and sugar syrup. Gin was the cocktail spirit of choice in nineteenth-century England. Over time the names John and Tom were used to identify the drink. Curiously, when made with whisky in Australia it was known as the Peter Collins. If it is made with bourbon it is the Colonel

Collins, the Mike Collins if made with Irish whiskey, the Sandy Collins when made with Scotch and, you guessed it, the Pedro Collins when rum is added.[8] This Tom Collins story is frequently cited in drink literature but it may be a work of fiction. In 1876 Jerry Thomas's *The Bartender's Guide* listed three Tom Collins drinks, each with the name of the base spirit following the drink name: Tom Collins whiskey, brandy and gin. He recommended that you 'imbibe [this drink] while it is lively'.[9]

The Daiquiri cocktail is said to take its name from the Daiquiri nickel mine in the Oriente province of Cuba.[10] Jennings Cox, an American mining engineer with Cuba's Spanish-American Iron Company is credited with inventing it in 1896 by adding lime juice and sugar to white rum. The person most closely identified with the Daiquiri is Constante Ribalagua who ran the bar at the La Floradita in Havana. This bar was called La Catedral del Daiquiri and Ribalagua the cocktail king – 'el rey de los coteleros'.[11] Ernest Hemingway was a frequent customer and his favourite drink was a double Daiquiri or Papa Dobles.[12]

Giuseppe Cipriani, the founder of Harry's Bar in Venice, invented the Bellini cocktail some time in the 1930s but did not name it until the 1948 exposition of the works of Italian Renaissance painter Giovanni Bellini. A Bellini is made from one part freshly squeezed white peach juice with three parts prosecco, an Italian version of champagne, and served in a well-chilled glass.[13]

Cipriani may have got his inspiration for the drink after seeing a Mimosa made. The Paris Ritz is frequently cited as the place where the Mimosa was invented in 1925. But it bears a striking resemblance to Buck's Fizz, an orange juice and champagne cocktail, named at the beginning of the Roaring Twenties for the club it was first served in. The combination of orange juice and champagne is still called a Buck's Fizz in England, while Mimosa is the preferred term in the USA and most of Europe.

Curiously, a whole class of cocktails have emerged for consumption at breakfast or brunch. Most of these drinks are compounded with vodka and orange, grapefruit, peach or cranberry juices, or fruit-flavoured liqueur. The fruity ingredients give the impression of getting your daily fruit and vitamin needs by consuming a Screwdriver, Sea Breeze, Melon Patch, Bellini or Mimosa with your eggs and bacon. Where a Martini with an olive could suggest that you might be abusing alcohol, a Mimosa made with orange juice, triple sec and champagne communicates that you are relaxing.

The quintessential morning drink is the Bloody Mary, a cocktail with French roots. It is known the world over for its curative effect on a hangover based upon the adage that the cure lies in 'a little of the hair of the dog that bit you'. It is a

Two bartenders tend a circular cocktail bar, c. 1935.

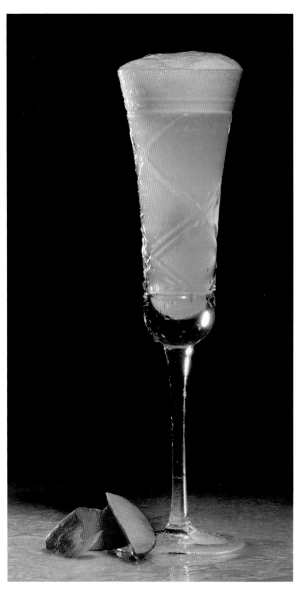

Bellini cocktail.

Glasses of Mimosa being served at a formal party.

drink to be enjoyed as you watch your omelette being assembled at the brunch table. This classic drink was concocted by bartender Fernand 'Pete' Petiot around 1920 at Harry's New York Bar in Paris. The drink was reportedly named for Mary 1 of England, who reigned for only five years (1553–8). 'Bloody' Mary earned her nickname because she had almost 300 people burned at the stake for heresy, including the Archbishop of Canterbury.

Fernand created his drink with vodka, which was available in Paris but still a stranger to America. This drink would have been impossible to make if canned tomato juice had not

Bloody Marys served outdoors at a tropical bar.

been introduced at the beginning of the twentieth century. Russian vodka and canned tomato juice was a marriage made in heaven. The arrival of US businessmen, tourists, soldiers and expatriates such as Ernest Hemingway guaranteed that the cocktail's fame would spread.

The Bloody Mary skipped across the pond when globe-trotting tycoon John Jacob Astor fell in love with the drink. He brought Fernand and his recipe to New York just after Prohibition to preside over the King Cole Bar at the St Regis Hotel. The Astors insisted that the drink be called the Red Snapper because they considered the original name too crude.

But people continued to order a Bloody Mary and its fame spread worldwide.[14] Ernest Hemingway, who had a vigorous taste for Bloody Marys, is quoted as saying, 'I introduced this drink to Hong Kong in 1941 and believe it did more than any other single factor except perhaps the Japanese Army to precipitate the fall of that Crown Colony.'[15]

Today there are many variations of this classic wake-me-upper. Made without alcohol it is the Virgin Mary, with tequila it is the Bloody Matador and if made with sake and flavoured with soy sauce and wasabe, it is the Bloody Maru. A non-alcoholic version appeared on American tables as the Tomato Juice Cocktail during the American period of Prohibition. This juice substitute was just fine in the homes of the middle class while oyster or crabmeat cocktails were the appetizer of choice in the homes of the well-to-do.[16]

Prawn cocktail illustration in a 1930s recipe booklet published by the Kelvinator Refrigerator Company.

Bloody Caesar cocktail made with Mott's Spicy Clamato Caesar (premixed bottle, celery, celery salt rim and ice).

In Yoko Ogawa's charming novel *The Housekeeper and the Professor* (2009), an intimate birthday party in modern Japan is described. Besides a cake decorated with chocolate-frosting, jelly bunnies and sugar angels, a 'rather plain' meal of 'shrimp cocktail, roast beef and mashed potatoes, spinach and bacon salad, pea soup, and fruit punch' was served.[17] Half a world and 200 years removed from its place of origin, the culinary offshoots of cocktails and punch are now global fare.

Almost every fruit, vegetable, herb or spice found on the planet has made it into a cocktail. Animal products have generally been absent but not totally ignored. Three exceptions are the Bullshot, Bloody Bull and Bloody Caesar. The Bullshot is a rather obscure cocktail, but it still survives in the international canon. Early recipes called for Campbell's condensed consommé, vodka, Worcestershire sauce and Tabasco.[18] Canadians are reported to use beef bouillon cubes in place of consommé.[19] A Bloody Mary made with beef broth is a Bloody Bull.[20]

Probably the most unlikely ingredient found in a cocktail is the humble clam – in the form of Clamato, a clam and tomato juice combination made by the Mott Company. This combination of tomatoes and clams seems strange, particularly from a company that made its name marketing apple juice. But then again, clam juice, with a dollop of whipped cream, was a popular restorative drink recommended for invalids in many nineteenth-century cookbooks. Mott's Clamato was introduced in California in 1969, the same year a restaurant owner in Calgary, Alberta, asked Walter Chell to create a signature cocktail. Using Clamato as his foundation, he created the Bloody Caesar with vodka, Clamato, Worcestershire sauce and a dash of Tabasco. Today it is Canada's number one cocktail with more than 200 million reportedly sold every year.[21] The Bloody Caesar is said to be very popular in the Caribbean and the Dominican Republic. When Clamato is mixed with tequila and hot sauce it is called a Clamato Tequila. With vodka, hot sauce, lime juice and beer it is a Tijuana Taxi.

The creation of cocktails was not limited to North America and Europe. With attention focused on British control of Hong Kong and the industrialization of Japan, it was inevitable that savvy bartenders would create cocktails at Asia's fashionable hotels and clubs. One of these creations was the Singapore Sling. It is believed that this was created by Ngiam Tong Boon, a Chinese bartender at the Long Bar of the Raffles Hotel in Singapore, around 1915. For a time it was also known as the Straits Sling. Made with gin, cherry brandy, Benedictine, bitters and lemon juice it had an attractive pink colour and may originally have been created to appeal to women.[22]

The most famous cocktail created in Australia is probably the Blow My Skull Off. It was concocted by Tasmania's hard-drinking Lieutenant Governor Thomas Davey, a captain of marines who fought at the Battle of Trafalgar in 1815. It was

The Mojito, along with other Latino cocktails, is currently enjoying a newfound popularity.

The Long Bar at the Raffles Hotel, Singapore.

A Pisco Sour. The froth on top is made by adding egg white to the drink before shaking.

composed of boiling water, sugar, lime or lemon juice, ale or porter, rum and brandy. In 1864 the recipe was printed in Australia's first cookbook: *The English and Australian Cookery Book* by Edward Abbott. Other ingredients that reportedly found their way into this explosive cocktail (or punch) were fortified wines, gin, claret, opium and cayenne pepper.[23]

Latin cocktails have been growing in popularity in recent years, not only in the USA due to the growth in its Latin population, but globally. Besides Daiquiris and Margaritas, the Mojito now has a firm footing at the bar. The American National Restaurant Association listed this minty libation as the third top beverage of the year behind energy drink cocktails and Martinis/flavoured Martinis.

The Mojito may get some strong competition from the Caipirinha, the national cocktail of Brazil. The Caipirinha is made with cachaça, muddled limes and sugar and served over ice. Cachaça is a complex spirit that has a rustic and earthy flavour and for some is an acquired taste. Caipirissima is made with rum instead of cachaça. If mixed with sake instead of cachaça, the drink is called Caipisake. Cachaça is distilled from sugar cane. It has long been associated with Brazil's slave culture and considered a drink for the poor. Brazil abolished slavery in 1888, the last country in the New World to do so. Brazil produces over 1.3 billion litres of cachaça each year, making it the third most distilled liquor behind vodka and Japanese *shochu*. A number of companies are selecting the best of Brazil's cachaça and sending it to France to be aged in used cognac casks.

Another Latin spirit that is catching the attention of mixologists is pisco, the national spirit of Peru. Pisco is technically a brandy since it is made by small artisan distillers from aromatic grapes using a copper pot still. Chile also produces a pisco but they use the vertical column still method. Surprisingly, pisco was the most popular spirit on America's West Coast – consumed in pisco punch and the Pisco Sour – between the time of the California Gold Rush and Prohibition. As testimony to its new popularity, a restaurant chain with 130 units in the USA has added the Pisco Sour to its drink menu, using pineapple juice instead of lemon or lime juice.[24]

The king of cocktails, the universal and iconic symbol of alcohol consumption, is the Martini. The Martini is more than a drink: it is a symbol of the culture of youth, fun, sex, upward mobility, corporate power and deal-making (two-Martini lunches), but at the same time it reflects maturity, education, sophistication, wealth and urban values. Nikita Khrushchev called the Martini 'America's lethal weapon'.[25]

The outline of a Martini glass fashioned from neon tubing is the universal symbol for the cocktail. When the outline of the V-shaped glass is placed within a red outlined circle, it is globally recognized as a sign that 'drinks are served here'. A red line through it means 'no drinking here'. A Martini would not be a Martini if it were not served in a V-shaped glass with a long stem. A Manhattan is served in its easily recognized highball glass and a Tom Collins in a tall glass. To serve an Old Fashioned in a Martini glass would be as silly as wearing pyjamas to the office. You could do it, of course, but you would look absurd. An Old Fashioned in a Martini glass is equally silly.

Casino Royale, the first of Ian Fleming's James Bond books, was published in 1953. The first drink Bond orders is a straight whisky on the rocks. Later on in the book he looks carefully at the barman and orders a drink:

> 'A dry martini', he said. 'One. In a deep champagne goblet.'
>
> 'Oui, monsieur.'
>
> 'Just a moment. Three measures of Gordon's, one of vodka, half a measure of Kina Lillet. Shake it very well until it's ice-cold, then add a large thick slice of lemon peel. Got it?'
>
> 'Certainly, monsieur.' The barman seemed pleased with the idea.

'Gosh that's certainly a drink', said Leiter.

Bond laughed. 'When I'm . . . er . . . concentrating', he explained, 'I never have more than one drink before dinner. But I do like that one to be large and very strong and very cold and very well-made. I hate small portions of anything, particularly when they taste bad. This drink's my own invention. I'm going to patent it when I can think of a good name.'

He watched carefully as the deep glass became frosted with the pale golden drink, slightly aerated by the bruising of the shaker. He reached for it and took a long sip.

'Excellent', he said to the barman, 'but if you can get a vodka made with grain instead of potatoes, you will find it still better.'[26]

Later on in the book he names the drink 'The Vesper' after the novel's lead female character, since 'It sounds perfect and it's very appropriate to the violet hour when my cocktail will now be drunk all over the world.'

The Martini is long overdue for an Oscar for the hundreds of bit parts it has played in setting the mood in Hollywood movies from the very beginning. It has been more than a stage prop. There is a memorable scene in *After Office Hours* (1935) when Clark Gable, holding a Martini in his left hand, tips it against Constance Bennett's Martini and they look deeply into each other's eyes. He is impeccably suave and she is a modern and sophisticated woman in a shimmering satin dress.[27]

5
The Social Side of the Cocktail

For most of the nineteenth century cocktails were viewed as a pre-dinner drink. By the end of that century the word 'cocktail' was reinterpreted to describe a non-alcoholic pre-dinner starter or appetizer. It was either a non-alcoholic beverage that mimicked a classic cocktail, or food – such as fruit or seafood – served in a cocktail glass. *The Twentieth Century Cook Book*, published in 1897, contained a recipe for 'oyster cocktail', which the author claimed was furnished 'by the chef of a prominent New York club'.[1]

The anti-saloon and Temperance movements in America during the 1920s influenced the popularity of these non-alcoholic cocktails. Thousands of inventive non-alcoholic cocktail recipes were published by Ladies' Aid Societies in cookbooks written to raise funds for church and community projects. Some mixed fruit drinks were given cocktail-sounding names such as 'Grapy Rickey' – a concoction of grape juice, lime juice, sugar and carbonated water.[2]

The church women who contributed recipes to fund-raising cookbooks clearly viewed cocktails made with any kind of alcohol as deleterious to both health and home. In order to tame these ungodly concoctions, contributors to these charity cookbooks invented so-called 'health cocktails'.

Two of these cocktails were submitted by the women of Cheshire, Connecticut, to *Recipes from Old Cheshire*, published in 1938.[3] One was composed of an egg yolk mixed with sugar and a combination of orange and lemon juice. Another called for prune juice, lemon juice, milk and sugar. But the health cocktail that pushed the boundary was the Castor Oil Cocktail, the recipe for which was published by the Marblehead Hospital Aid Association in 1958. This cocktail was made by beating two tablespoons of castor oil with a tumbler of orange juice and baking soda.[4]

The prominent mention of clam cocktail on the signboard of Stillman's eatery, next to a smaller sign for 'near beer', a low-alcohol beer permitted during Prohibition, may have been a coded message to customers that more than clams, namely real cocktails, could be had at this eatery.

Stillman's clam shack may have been serving more than clams during Prohibition.

It would be seafood cocktails, served in V-shaped Martini glasses, or fruit cocktails, served in sherbet glasses (ice cream glassware that imitates cocktail stemware), which became firmly embedded during the twentieth century as a separate course at formal American dinners. Based upon published recipes, the most popular food cocktail was the oyster cocktail. This dish was constructed by nesting a few freshly shucked oysters in a Martini glass, topping them with a dollop of ketchup seasoned with Tabasco and Worcestershire sauce, and garnishing with a lemon wedge. During the twentieth century, with the introduction of reliable refrigerators in the home, crabmeat, clams and eventually cooked shrimp would be added to the seafood repertoire. For most Americans today it is the shrimp cocktail (in the UK known as the prawn cocktail), made with a shellfish perfectly designed by nature to hang off the edge of a cocktail glass, that is the quintessential first course.

In more modest restaurants, at wedding banquets and in the home, it was the fruit cocktail that ruled. This cocktail was made from chunks of mixed seasonal fruit topped with a maraschino cherry dyed bright red with the chemical red dye no. 2. Because of a fear that this dye might cause cancer, it was replaced with red dye no. 40. The simplest solution would have been to abandon the cherry but, in the mind of most people, it was as essential to the fruit cocktail as it was to the Manhattan.

Hundreds of fundraising cookbooks published by church ladies during the Prohibition era contain recipes for cocktail appetizers, Temperance punches, coolers and rickeys; an effort, no doubt, by these very prim and proper ladies to demonstrate that they were not totally divorced from mainline eating and drinking trends. Of course, these Prohibition drinks did not contain alcohol. In the same vein, and with a smile and a wink, these same ladies slipped into church cookbooks their recipes for devilled eggs, devil's food cake and devilled (meaning highly seasoned) ham sandwiches.

Prohibition in America during the 1920s forced men out of saloons and taprooms into speakeasies (the word derives from the practice of speaking softly when trying to gain entrance to these illegal drinking establishment). All along the coast bootleggers delivered illegal bottled alcohol from Canada and Mexico and from ships at anchor in international waters. While a man would not think of taking a woman to a neighbourhood bar or taproom to order a legal drink, they did not hesitate to break the law by taking their wives or girlfriends to a speakeasy, and women were known to sneak out of the home for an afternoon there.

Crime novelist Elmore Leonard used cocktails as a literary device to set the time and mood in his novel *The Hot Kid* (2005), which takes place during the heyday of the speakeasy. Kitty, one of the characters, works as a cocktail waitress wearing only a teddy. Leonard's fans appreciate his carefully researched settings and details such as the Sidecar (made with cognac, orange liqueur and lemon juice) she served to 'three young hotshots at a table in the bar, bringing them each two cocktails at a time so they wouldn't die of thirst between drinks'.[5] In another scene the girlfriend of the federal marshal prepares a Tom Collins for each of them, hers with a cherry and his without. This cocktail is not as popular today but sets the scene before the Second World War.

Following Prohibition, which ended in 1933, the cocktail lounge came into prominence as a social gathering place. The cocktail lounge and the art deco style were a perfect match. In America's leading hotels large spaces were decorated and engineered to create a space for seeing and being seen. These rooms were carefully organized spaces with small tables and

Postcard of the cocktail lounge at the Mayflower Hotel, Washington, DC, first opened in 1925.

potted plants to add a casual garden effect; a grand piano and rich architectural detail all contributed to an atmosphere of pampered service. These rooms were ideally designed for sipping cocktails but were not large enough for dinner. The cocktail lounge in the Mayflower Hotel, which promoted itself as the finest hotel in the nation's capital, was typical of cocktail lounges just before the Second World War. On the back of a postcard, the sender, attending a Daughters of the American Revolution (DAR) conference, urged her friend 'to come on down and have a cocktail with me in this beautiful room'.

Mystery novels written in the 1940s and '50s often featured private detectives and reporters who were depicted as tough characters and consummate cocktail drinkers, such as Raymond Chandler's Philip Marlowe and Dashiell Hammett's Sam Spade. When these novels were made into movies producers frequently filmed these characters with a cocktail in hand in dingy smoke-filled bars, taprooms or Las Vegas casinos. These casinos still maintain a strict dress code when it

Postcard of the Mermaid Lounge at the Hotel Alms, Cincinatti, Ohio, *c.* 1950s.

comes to cocktail waitresses. They hire women exclusively to serve cocktails, preferably 'young, shapely, smiling and thin' ones, and dress them in alluring form-fitting and sexually provocative uniforms. Their role is to please the male casino customer and maintain the casino's glamorous illusion. The cocktail waitress is part of the fantasy and entertainment offered to casino customers.[6]

But cocktails were also drunk in the home: the cocktail party evolved in America during the twentieth century. Middle-class families found that they could afford to entertain at home with drinks and finger food, especially since these events were restricted to a small number of people and generally lasted only between the hours of 5:00 and 8:00 p.m.

After the Second World War the cocktail party was re-invented as a way of entertaining business associates at home. Bringing the boss home for cocktails and dinner was a frequent TV plot played out in numerous US situation comedies such as *I Love Lucy*.

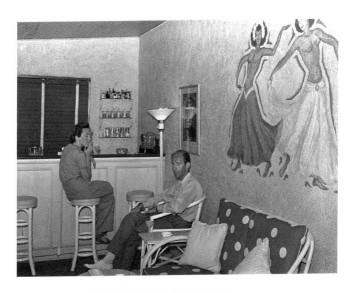

Wealthy Americans adopted the cocktail habit in bars built in their own houses, like this one in the home of the former president of the Gillette razor blade company, Florida, 1939.

Marilyn Monroe and Joe DiMaggio after their wedding, 14 January 1954.

In George Price's cartoon from the *New Yorker* of *c.* 1971, a housewife wearing a 'bunny' cocktail outfit greets her husband with a drink as he enters the front door.

The cocktail hour created a fashion problem for women since tea-time or dinner attire was not chic enough for sipping naughty afternoon Martinis. Out of this need the cocktail dress emerged, along with other items of apparel that complemented this new culture. In 1999 Sotheby's auctioned off 161 lots of cocktail-related items including cocktail dresses, suits and ensembles. The auction's star piece was the cocktail suit worn by Marilyn Monroe at her wedding to Joe DiMaggio. This brown wool suit with white mink collar and rhinestone buttons was estimated to fetch up to $20,000. The auction also had a emerald green Playboy bunny costume (bust 36 inches, waist 23 inches, US size 4–6) with ears,

Cornell Capa, *Literary Cocktail Party at George Plimpton's Upper East Side Apartment, New York City*, 1963.

tail, collar, cuffs, cuff links and bow tie. This was worn by waitresses in Playboy Clubs, and was the first work uniform ever to be granted trademark protection by the US Patent and Trademark Office.[7]

The woman of the house, in the new role of hostess, turned to the cocktail dress, a knee-length sleeveless outfit that fanned out as an inverted V. When viewed abstractly, it takes the shape of a Martini glass turned upside down. In time the cocktail dress became a sheath that is still in fashion.

It was in the 1950s that women invented the cocktail apron to give the illusion of being the perfect hostess. These aprons were not the practical and functional attire worn by their mothers in the kitchen. Cocktail aprons were frequently constructed from ruffled nylon and were shorter and much sassier. (One notable violation of the cocktail dress protocol is the dress code, or lack thereof, at a Jimmy Buffet

Margaritaville concert. Concertgoers, called Parrot Heads, are known for their outrageous, provocative and preposterous Caribbean costumes and their cocktails.)

Peanuts served in small bowls at cocktail receptions became known as cocktail peanuts. Finger foods served at these events were called cocktail hors d'oeuvres or appetizers. They were passed around by a uniformed cocktail waitress or waiters, among those who could afford the expense, or by the hostess in more modest households. As a rule cocktail food and drink is taken while standing and socializing is expected. A cocktail singer or piano player might provide soft music to facilitate conversation.

With cocktail culture, the hors d'oeuvre took on a new meaning. Once a small portion of highly seasoned food that preceded a meal, it became an essential part of cocktail parties. Lucy G. Allen noted this trend in her cookbook *A*

Sandy Skoglund, *The Cocktail Party*, 1992, installation made with Cheez Doodles embedded in epoxy resin. *The Cocktail Party* © 1992 Sandy Skoglund.

THE SHERATON-BILTMORE HOTEL
Providence, Rhode Island

Postcard of cocktail waitresses at the Sheraton-Biltmore Hotel, Providence, Rhode Island, 1950s.

John Sloan, *A Thirst for Art*, 1939, etching.

Book of Hors d'Oeuvres (1941). She found that hors d'oeuvres 'have grown tremendously in popularity and are now used to accompany cocktails'.[8] Any host could pull together a successful cocktail party with hors d'oeuvres, she claimed, because all that was needed was 'imagination, plus whatever happens to be on the shelves of the refrigerator'. She stated that the 'cocktail canapé' was the most popular and defined a canapé as a savoury mixture placed upon a firm edible base, preferably toasted or fried bread, with the crust removed and cut into 'round, oval, crescent, diamond or palm-leaf shapes'.[9] Skewered titbits were also popular, giving rise to the cocktail pick.

The cocktail party helped people who were not acquainted to enter into effortless banter and possibly even develop lasting friendships. William Grimes, restaurant critic for the *New York Times* and author of *Straight Up or on the Rocks*, found 'the cocktail party more often than not a gathering of near-strangers brought together in a setting of false intimacy'.[10] Cocktail parties soon became an established institution among

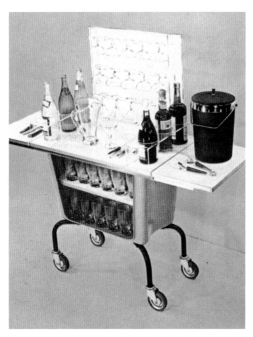

Postcard of a drinks trolley, 1950s.

politicians, diplomats and lobbying groups. Making the round of Washington's many cocktail parties is viewed as necessary for making contacts, being seen, raising funds and gaining introductions. Corporate and political cocktail parties are so important globally that they have created an industry of catering companies that specialize in the art of the cocktail party.

Not all cocktail parties are created equal, as Mr Brown, the protagonist in Graham Greene's novel *The Comedians* (1966), was to learn during his sojourn in Port-au-Prince, Haiti.[11] He discovered that as an owner of a less than luxury hotel, he was invited to cocktail parties of the 'second-class order'. First-class parties, 'where caviare was served', were reserved for diplomats, ambassadors and ministers. Third-class cocktail parties were held out of a sense of 'duty'.

Sidecar cocktail with orange garnish.

The popularity of cocktail parties waned after the counterculture movement of the 1960s. But, according to cocktail party scholar Leslie Brenner, the 1990s witnessed a resurgence of the venue because young people 'found the kitsch value of cocktail culture appealing'.[12] Cocktail parties became popular ways of opening exhibitions or galleries, launching a new book or product, breaking the ice at conferences or celebrating a promotion or retirement.

Colourful and Children's Cocktails

During America's colonial period drinking spirits was primarily reserved for men. For most of America's history women had limited access to alcoholic beverages. They did not frequent taverns and inns where alcoholic beverages were served except when travelling. Women risked being identified as 'loose' if they entered a bar or saloon but they did entertain their friends with fortified wines such as port, sherry and Madeira and an occasional brandy for their health. The first cocktails were not gender-neutral. Since they were made from 'hard liquors' they were a man's drink.

It was at speakeasies and cocktail parties that women were introduced to hard liquor. In 1934 an article in the *New Era Illustrated* noted that women were consuming more spirits than in the past. To assure them that there was nothing socially or medically wrong with the consumption of alcohol, the magazine told them that gin was 'recommended' for women by the medical community. Furthermore, alcohol was widely prescribed by the medical community for its 'beneficial effects on disorders such as gout, rheumatism and any form of bladder or kidney complaints'. The article confirmed that 'women have for many years appreciated the necessity of

Two Typical Kentuckians, Personality and Mint Julep, Relics Almost Extinct, 1951, postcard.

Cosmopolitans, often considered a woman's drink.

taking gin as a remedy for the minor ailments to which their sex is subject'.[13]

Many of the cocktails invented in the early twentieth century were concocted to appeal to the visual and sensory taste of women. With some exceptions, men tend to favour cocktails that run the spectrum of natural wood colours from dark mahogany, maple, walnut, tan and blond to the clarity of a Martini. When large numbers of women began to consume spirits during Prohibition, it was soon recognized that they preferred more colourful drinks.

This 'cocktail gender divide' is still very real today. The LeBar at Chicago's Sofitel Water Tower Hotel developed a cocktail menu labelled 'Liquid Suggestions'. 'His' cocktails are described as 'Willful Beverages both Handsome and Refined' while 'Hers' are 'Downright Gorgeous Cocktails Demonstrating both Elegance and Complexity'. As author Dara Moskowitz Grumdahl observed in *Gourmet* magazine, it would require a man of considerable courage and self assurance to saunter up to the bar and order a 'Raspberry Womanhattan'.[14] A Boston magazine asked a number of bartenders to share the 'snap judgments' they make of an individual when they order a specific drink. A Cosmopolitan drinker 'is definitely a girl', said one bartender, and another said she is probably 'put together quite well as far as their outfit goes'. 'Sloppily' dressed people do not order a Cosmo. Gin and tonic drinkers are men '75 per cent of the time', said one bartender, 'a guy's guy'. As for people who order a Manhattan, one bartender said that he 'rarely 'serves Manhattans

L to R: Ruth Ray, Dottie Berg, Gally O'Brien and Rose Lee celebrate the end of Prohibition at the National Liquor Convention held at the Stevens Hotel, Chicago, 11 March 1935.

Mai Tai. Both Don the Beachcomber and Trader Vic's claim to have invented this cocktail.

to women'. Another said it more bluntly: 'it's a man's drink', a drink for a 'tough-guy'.[15]

But the last thing a 'tough-guy' wants in his cocktail is a cocktail umbrella, unless he is sitting on the beach in the Caribbean or at a hotel pool bar. This silly and frivolous cocktail garnish is reported to have first been used at the Don the Beachcomber 'tiki' restaurant in Hollywood in the 1930s. This exotic and playful symbol of Asia was soon copied by San Francisco's Polynesian-style restaurant chain, Trader Vic's.

When parents order cocktails at a restaurant or an event at which children are present it is only natural for the child to

A Shirley Temple.

want a drink that is just as colourful and grown-up looking. To meet this need the Shirley Temple was born. Mock cocktails, drinks with the look of the real thing but without spirits, have been received with enthusiastic applause by adults as well as children. But the mocktail, as some call it, is not for sissies. It must possess its own intensity and consist of ingredients that will encourage sipping. According to Boston drink expert Jackson Cannon, it must 'affect the body like that preprandial drink should'.[16] Mocktails, because they are free of alcohol, are ideal to sell at university-sponsored theme events in America, where most college students are below legal drinking age, and can be a welcome change from the traditional carbonated beverages served at restaurants, weddings and other special events.

'Cocktails' in Wider Culture

In the twentieth century the word 'cocktail' attached itself as a prefix to everything it touched, even the clothing and jewellery (cocktail dress, cocktail ring and so on) worn by the drinker. Small talk over a cocktail became 'cocktail conversations' or 'cocktail whispers', as lasting as alcohol fumes. Ethan Canin's *America America* (2008), his election-year novel about Henry Bonwiller, a senator and flawed presidential candidate, used the term 'cocktail whispers' three times to emphasize how damaging information can be ignited on Washington's cocktail circuit, where diplomats and bureaucrats mingle.

The word 'cocktail' creates such a powerful visual image that people began to use the word as an adjective to describe almost anything that was a mixture of explosive and potentially destructive ingredients. In 1940 an incendiary device consisting of gasoline in a wine bottle with a cloth wick was named a 'Molotov cocktail' after Vyacheslav Molotov, who had claimed that the Soviet Union was not dropping bombs on Finland but was instead delivering food to starving Finns. The Finns started to refer to the Soviet bombs jokingly as 'Molotov bread baskets' and responded in kind by attacking Soviet tanks with 'Molotov cocktails', a drink to go with the food.[17]

In 2009 a Boston newspaper announced on the front page that a 'Winter Cocktail', meaning a mix of snow, sleet and rain, was scheduled to hit the eastern half of the country.[18] The many medications taken by HIV patients are sometimes called a 'drug cocktail'. Contaminants in a water supply are a

This English home guardsman is holding a 'Molotov cocktail'. It's really a homemade anti-tank grenade and he is about to toss it during a training session, 1940.

'toxic cocktail', just like secondhand smoke. Researchers talk about creating a prophylactic cocktail or antibiotic cocktail to fight bacterial infections. Newspapers have referred to the potentially deadly combination of alcohol and prescription medication as a toxic cocktail. The *New York Post* in 2008 noted that pop idol Britney Spears consumed a 'Purple Monster', made of vodka, Nyquil and Red Bull, followed by a toxic cocktail of sleeping pills, Vicodin, Ritalin and Zantac.[19] ABC News reported that celebrity Anna Nicole Smith died from a drug cocktail composed of antidepressants, anti-anxiety drugs and chloral hydrate, among others.[20] Chloral hydrate, also known as 'knockout drops', was used by a Chicago bartender to put in his patrons' drinks before he robbed them. This debilitating cocktail was called a 'Mickey Finn'.

Cocktails in the Future

What is the future of the cocktail? Mintel, an international market research firm, predicts that mocktails will be a hot restaurant trend. Mintel claims that there is a market for better tasting and more sophisticated non-alcoholic drinks, such as ice-cold lemonade with strawberry purée, fresh ginger and crushed mint leaves.[21] Besides non-alcoholic options, hospitality industry experts anticipate that Mojitos and Caipirinhas, to name two, will be fashionable, along with pomegranate drinks, seasonal berries and Asian flavours such as green tea and lychee.[22]

In Japan *shochu* (show-chew), a single pot distilled beverage, is receiving considerable attention and eating into the sake market. It can be made from barley, rice or even sweet potatoes. In addition to yeast the microbe koji (Aspergillus mould) is used in the fermentation process, and the distillate is aged in barrels. When mixed with water it is called a 'water cocktail'.[23] In 2003 the consumption of *shochu* in Japan surpassed that of sake for the first time in 53 years.[24] Bartenders are sure to give this versatile beverage their serious attention.

With globalization it is only natural that China will be promoting cocktails made from its national spirits. At the top of the list is *maotai*, a clear liquor made from sorghum and barley. Originally reserved for diplomatic banquets it is sure to end up in endless cocktail concoctions now that it is being promoted for export. Other Chinese liquors – such as *fen chiew*, made from sorghum; *kwai fa can chiew*, a liqueur made from grapes with a soft cinnamon taste; and *chu yeh ching chiew*, a herbal liqueur with an aroma of dried apricot and a hint of anise – are all candidates for the magic of mixologists.[25]

To discover the perfect cocktail, an international cocktail mixing contest was held at the London headquarters of the International Geneva Association. Experts from all parts of the world competed.

The availability of superior small-batch artisan-made spirits and high-end gin, vodka and tequilas along with new spirits such as Brazilian cachaças and Peruvian piscos offer unlimited possibilities for bartenders and their clientele. Expect to see artisan liquors, even vitamin-fortified energy cocktails, promoted at trendy lounges.[26]

Beverage experts predict that the current trends for natural, healthy and organic foods will be applied to drinks too. The farm-to-table ethical discussion about free-range chickens, fair trade coffee, sustainable agriculture and food miles – the distance foods have travelled to your table – is spilling into the bar: expect to find cocktails made with organic, seasonal, local and sustainable ingredients and christened with environmentally friendly-sounding names.[27] The Nacional 27, a Latin restaurant in Chicago, serves a 'healthy cocktail' called the 'Look Better Naked Margarita' made with ingredients including organic salt and organic green peppercorns.

In this still from *Cocktail* (dir. Roger Donaldson, 1988), Tom Cruise demonstrates the art of flair bartending.

When two men are behind the bar competing for tips it is inevitable that one bartender will challenge the other's speed, dexterity, knowledge and accuracy in pouring drinks. When bartenders started juggling liquor bottles with choreographed dance moves for the entertainment of their customers, 'flair bartending' was born. The film *Cocktail* (1988), with the image of Tom Cruise flipping bottles, ushered in a dramatic increase in flair bartending competitions. Organized bartending competitions have a long history in Europe, as evidenced from a photograph from a 1940 competition in England. But flair bartending in the USA can only be traced back to the TGI Friday restaurant chain in the 1970s. John J. B. Bandy, the winner of the first TGI Friday's Bar Olympics, choreographed and trained Tom Cruise for the big screen.

Today's new breed of bartender is a 'bar chef' who will create a cocktail in front of you or at your table from locally grown ingredients. These may include freshly made bitters and organic spirits made by an artisan alchemist. As this talented mixologist – or cocktail performer – entertains his or her

Modern cocktail served at the Match Bar, London.

customer, he or she instructs them on the ingredients and the story behind the drink's creation. In many of America's fine-dining restaurants there is no shortage of customers willing to pay premium prices for this attentive and professional bar service.[28] Writing in the beverage trade publication *Santé*, Jacques Bezuidenhout observed that this is forcing some bartenders who take their craft seriously to attend spirits and cocktail seminars in order to stay at the top of their game.[29]

Another trend to watch is the pairing of cocktail culture and fine dining. At a few restaurants the bartender and executive chef team up to customize a multicourse meal highlighted by an interactive cocktail demonstration with 'stories about the drinks' histories'.[30] At New Orleans Café Adelaide and The Swizzle Stick Bar, beef short ribs osso bucco might be paired at the chef's table with a Derby Cocktail made with bourbon, sweet vermouth, orange liqueur, lime juice and mint.

Talented bartenders are now mixologists and some have star power comparable to that of celebrity chefs. They travel the world holding classes, lecturing at trade conferences and exchanging ideas with peers. This new breed will create their own drink infusions, homemade bitters, made-from-scratch juices and mixes and will even push the envelope with liquid nitrogen-aided preparations.[31]

A barman at work.

Recipes

The two cocktails below are from *The Ideal Bartender* by Tom Bullock, the first African-American to write a cocktail book. First published in 1917, it was republished in 2001 by the Howling at the Moon Press. For a quarter of a century Mr Bullock plied his craft at the St Louis Country Club. Here he met George Herbert Walker, grandfather and great-grandfather respectively of the 41st and 43rd presidents of the USA. Mr Walker wrote the introduction to this small volume of pre-Prohibition cocktails.

Absinthe Cocktail

Fill mixing glass ¾ full Shaved Ice.
½ jigger Water.
½ jigger Absinthe.
2 dashes Angostura Bitters.
1 teaspoonful Benedictine.

Stir; strain into Cocktail glass and serve.

Black Stripe

Pour Wineglass Santa Cruz or Jamaica Rum into a small Bar glass and add 1 tablespoonful of Molasses. If to serve hot, fill glass with boiling Water and sprinkle Nutmeg on top. If to serve cold, add ½ Wineglass Water. Stir well and fill up with Shaved Ice.

Pousse Café
–from Charles Ranhofer, *The Epicurean* (1894)

The pousse café is a drink composed of four kinds of liquor of different colour; that is to say, white cream of peppermint, green Chartreuse, cream of cocoa and brandy. These four liquors are poured into a glass tumbler in such a way that they remain in distinct layers, which is done by carefully pouring the above liquors, one after the other, against the side of the glass; thus the liquors flow down gently without mixing.

Gin Rickey

Following America's experiment with Prohibition, some drinkers had to be reacquainted with the full galaxy of cocktail possibilities. To meet this need a score of cocktail books were published in the 1930s to meet a renewed interest in cocktail culture. In 1934 Magnus Bedenbek, a newspaper editor, wrote *What Shall We Drink?* to help Americans regain the almost forgotten art of making a legal drink. The instructions below are from a chapter devoted to a class of cocktails called 'Rickeys'.

First let's get acquainted with Mr Gin Rickey, who was the most popular member of the family long ago.

Into our individual thin goblets put a few cubes of ice or cracked ice, as preferred. Pour into each glass about two ounces (60 ml) of dry or sweet gin. Most men prefer the sweet for a Rickey. Now squeeze into each glass a half lime and let the lime drop after its juice into each glass. Um-m!

Now get that Vichy or seltzer bottle and send a stream of effervescent fluid into the glass until it nearly touches the rim.

Ah, that's it! Now stir it with a spoon and let's toast each other! If you like it stronger, add more Gin.

Mint Julep

The julep is a class of drinks made from bourbon, sugar, water and a sprig of fresh spearmint that originated in the Southern states of America. Harry Craddock, the London author of *The Savoy Cocktail Book* (1930), claims that Captain Frederick Marryat, seaman and novelist, introduced the mint julep to the British Isles. The following recipe is from *Dishes and Beverages of the Old South* (1913) by Martha McCulloch-Williams.

This requires the best of everything if you would have it in perfection. Especially the mint and the whiskey or brandy. Choose tender, quick-grown mint, leafy, not long-stalked and coarse, wash it very clean, taking care not to bruise it in the least, and lay in a clean cloth upon ice. Chill the spirits likewise. Put the sugar and water in a clean fruit jar, and set on ice. Do this at least six hours before serving so the sugar shall be fully dissolved. Four lumps to the large goblet is about right – with half a gobletful of fresh cold water. At serving time, rub a zest of lemon around the rim of each goblet – the goblets must be well chilled – then half fill with the dissolved sugar, add a tablespoonful of cracked ice, and stand sprigs of mint thickly all around the rim. Set the goblets in the tray, then fill up with whiskey or brandy or both, mixed – the mixture is best with brands that blend smoothly. Drop in the middle a fresh ripe strawberry, or cherry, or slice of red peach, and serve at once. Fruit can be left out without harm to flavor – it is mainly for the satisfaction of the eye . . . To get the real old-time effect, serve with spoons in the goblets rather than straws. In dipping and sipping more of the mint-essence comes out – beside the clinking of the spoons is nearly as refreshing as the tinkle of the ice.

Manhattan Cocktail

–from Charles Ranhofer, *The Epicurean* (1894)

Place some very finely broken ice in a large glass, add a third of a glassful of whiskey and two-thirds of vermouth, also one dash of Boker's bitters; mix properly, strain and serve in small glasses.

Martini

The following recipe for a Martini is typical for the period. It was published in a generic collection of cocktail recipes called *Bottoms UP . . . Guide to Pleasant Drinking*, distributed by the First Avenue Wine & Liquor Corp of New York City to their customers in 1949. Throughout the 1950s and 1960s the ratio of vermouth to gin continued to change, from 3-to-2 to 5-to-1 to 8-to-1 to pure gin and a whisper of vermouth swirled around the glass.

1 Dash Orange Bitters
½ oz (15 ml) French Vermouth
½ oz (15 ml) Italian Vermouth
1 ½ oz (45 ml) Dry Gin

Stir well with cracked ice, strain into 3 oz. (90 ml) Cocktail glass. Serve with an Olive.

Brandy, Whiskey, Holland Gin and Tom Gin Cocktails

–from Charles Ranhofer, *The Epicurean* (1894)

Charles Ranhofer was the chef at Delmonico's restaurant in New York City for almost 34 years. Delmonico's hosted many dignitaries including Charles Dickens and US presidents Andrew Johnson and Ulysses S. Grant. In 1894 Ranhofer published *The Epicurean*, an encyclopaedic treatise on food and food service. The following cocktail recipes are from his monumental work.

Put some very finely broken ice in a large glass, add a glassful either of brandy, whiskey or Holland gin, one dash of Boker's bitters, and two dashes of sweetening (gum syrup); mix well together with a spoon, strain and serve in small glasses. Tom gin cocktail is made exactly the same, only using old Tom gin and suppressing the sweetening.

Cosmopolitan

In Benjamin Black's (pen name of Irish writer John Banville) 2008 novel *The Lemur*, set in the last decade of the twentieth century, the character John Glass finds his mistress Alison standing at the bar, 'holding a tall glass of something crimson'. Presumably it was a Cosmopolitan, a rather new cocktail and a favourite drink among women. John ordered a dry Martini, the male equivalent to her feminine drink. Alison looked at his drink and 'arched an eyebrow'. The following recipe is from Salvatore Calabrese's 1997 book *Classic Cocktails*.

1¾ ounces vodka
⅓ ounce Cointreau
⅓ ounce cranberry juice
⅓ ounce fresh lime juice

Pour into shaker and shake. Strain to glass and garnish with a twist of lime.

Fish House Punch

Fish House Punch is possibly the most frequently celebrated punch found in American drink anthologies and has always been associated with the city of Philadelphia. The following recipe was contributed by Col. M. Richards Mucklé of Philadelphia to the *Colonial Receipt Book*, a fundraising cookbook published in 1907 to support the work of the Hospital of the University of Pennsylvania in Philadelphia.

Put 1 gallon of boiling water on 8 pounds of lump sugar, and dissolve it to a clear syrup. Then add ½ gallon of lemon juice. When sufficiently cooled add 1 gallon of brandy, ½ gallon of Jamaica rum, 1 pint of peach brandy. If in season, put in a pine-apple sliced. If not in season, a couple of sliced oranges, or some strawberries will do. If you want a potent punch, add a gallon of champagne, if a light punch, put 2 gallons instead of 1 of boiling water on the sugar. Some people add green tea leaves to the mixture, which in my opinion is an abomination. A larger or smaller quantity may be made by increasing or decreasing the quantity of the ingredients in the same proportion as above.

Cocktails around the Globe

In this era of globalization, tourist and business travellers demand certain minimum standards when it comes to accommodation and food and drink. They expect and demand, whether they are in New York City, Mumbai or Hanoi, flushing toilets, a hot shower, a memorable meal and a cold Martini.

To accommodate the travelling public, hotel bars, cafes and restaurants in every country have created a galaxy of invented cocktails using indigenous spirits and ingredients. Yet many cocktails which appear to have been invented in a specific country may actually have been created thousands of miles away as part of a theme party or as a signature cocktail for a new restaurant.

To find a cocktail that meets your cultural, ethnic or national desires, go to your favourite online search engine and type in the desired parameters – country, alcohol and so on – and you will be amazed at the results. The following is just a brief sip of the constellation of cocktails from around the globe.

Australia

Lychee Caprioska: vodka with lime slice and lychees crushed with palm sugar
Barrier Reef: Cointreau, Angostura bitters, blue curaçao and vanilla ice cream
South Pacific: Gin Galliano, lemonade and blue curaçao

Russia

Cossack Crush Martini: Russian vodka, pomegranate juice, grenadine, limoncello with a kumquat for garnish

China

China Blue: a popular drink in Taiwan, Japan and China made with lychee liqueur, grapefruit juice and blue curaçao

Japan

Blushing Geisha: sake, midori (Melon Liqueur), Malibu strawberry liqueur with a fresh strawberry for garnish

Korea

Fallen Angel: soju (clear spirit made from rice, with or without sweet potatoes), green crème de menthe, lemon juice, Angostura bitters with a maraschino cherry garnish

Puerto Rico

Pina Colada: mix of white and dark rum, coconut cream, pineapple juice, Angostura bitters. Garnished with whipped cream, a maraschino cherry and a pineapple slice

Cuba

Mango Daiquiri: dark rum, orange curaçao liqueur, mango chunks and sweet and sour mix with ice in a blender

Spain

SherryTinni: gin, manzanilla or fino sherry and manzanilla olives

South Africa

Elephant's Mudbath: vodka, crème de cacao (brown) and Amarula Cream (South African cream liqueur)

Italy

Sgroppino: prosecco (Italian sparkling white wine), vodka, frozen lemon sorbet and fresh mint leaves

Norway

Nordic Dame: akvavit (distilled spirit flavoured with caraway seeds), brown crème de cacao and cream

Thailand

Bangkok Cooler: Sam Som (Thai whiskey), crème de menthe (green), lime juice, grenadine and pineapple juice

Vietnam

Saigon Girl: vodka, midori (melon liqueur), blue curaçao, orange and lemon juice
Phantini: equal amounts of gin and vodka and a dash of *nuoc nam* (fish sauce)

Brazil

Caipirinha: cachaça (from fermented sugar cane) with lime crushed with sugar

Mexico

Tequila Twist: tequila (blue-agave-based spirit), lime and orange juice, sugar and a strawberry garnish

References

1 The Mysterious Birth of the Cocktail

1   Aristotle, *Materiology*, Bk. II, Ch. II. Quoted in George H. Jackson, *The Medicinal Value of French Brandy* (Montreal, 1928), p. 131.

2   In Tom Standage, *A History of the World in Six Glasses* (New York, 2005), p. 99.

3   Harvey W. Wiley, *Beverages and Their Adulteration* (Philadelphia, PA, 1919), p. 375.

4   Ernest L. Abel, '*Gin Lane*: Did Hogarth Know about Fetal Alcohol Syndrome?', *Alcohol and Alcoholism*, XXXVI/2 (2001), pp. 131–4.

5   Jonathan Swift, *Gulliver's Travels* (New York, 1970), p. 219.

6   William Grimes, *Straight Up or on the Rocks: The Story of the American Cocktail* (New York, 2001), pp. 39–40.

7   In John Ciardi, *A Browser's Dictionary and Native's Guide to the Unknown American Language* (New York, 1980), p. 84.

8   In Grimes, *Straight Up or on the Rocks*, p. 42.

9   Jeri Quinzio, 'Cocktails', in *Encyclopedia of Food and Culture*, ed. Solomon H. Katz, vol. 1 (New York, 2003), pp. 425–8.

10 *Samuel Johnson's Dictionary: Selections from the 1755 Work That Defined the English Language*, ed. Jack Lynch (Delray Beach, FL, 2002), p. 112.

11 Harry Botsford, 'The Genesis and Natural History of the Cocktail', *Cabaret*, I/11 (16 March 1956).

12 Jeri Quinzio, *Of Sugar and Snow: A History of Ice Cream Making* (Berkeley, CA, 2009), p. 122.

2 Punch, the Cocktail's Original Ancestor

1 Joseph M. Carlin, 'Punch', in *The Oxford Encyclopedia of Food and Drink in America*, ed. Andrew F. Smith (Oxford, 2004), pp. 332–3.
2 'Edward Vernon', Wikipedia, available at http://en.wikipedia.org/wiki/Edward_Vernon, accessed May 2011.
3 James J. McDonald, *Life in Old Virginia* (Norfolk, VA, 1907), p. 303.
4 Nicks Wine Merchants, 'Drinking Vessels of Bygone Days', available at www.nicks.com.au, accessed May 2011.
5 Joyce W. Carlo, *Trammels, Trenchers, and Tartlets: A Definitive Tour of the Colonial Kitchen* (Old Saybrook, CT, 1982), p. 117.
6 'Alcoholic Punch Drink and Recipe', available at www.2020site.org, accessed May 2011.
7 Elisabeth Seeley, recipe for 'Connecticut Colonial Punch', in Fairfield County Republican Women's Association, *Ye Tercentenary Cook Book* (Fairfield, CT, 1935), p. 9.
8 Philip Chadwick Foster Smith, *Crystal Blocks of Yankee Coldness*, Wenham Historical Association and Museum, August 1962. Reprinted from Essex Institute Historical collections, July 1961, The Essex Institute, Salem, MA.
9 *Illustrated London News*, VI (17 May 1845), pp. 315–16, cited in Smith, *Crystal Blocks of Yankee Coldness*, p. 25.
10 Wilmer and Smith, *European Times*, 1845, cited in Smith, *Crystal Blocks of Yankee Coldness*, p. 21.

3 American Taverns, the Cocktail's Nursery

1 Joseph M. Carlin, 'Bars', in *The Oxford Encyclopedia of Food and Drink in America* (Oxford and New York, 2004), pp. 67–9.

2 Quoted in William Grimes, *Straight Up or on the Rocks: The Story of the American Cocktail* (New York, 2001), p. 60.

3 Madelon Powers, *Faces Along the Bar: Lore and Order in the Workingman's Saloon, 1870–1920* (Chicago and London, 1998), p. 138.

4 Ibid., p. 86.

5 William F. Mulhall, 'The Golden Age of Booze', in *Valentine's Manual of Old New York*, ed. H. C. Brown, n.s., no. 7 (New York, 1923).

6 T. S. Arthur, *Ten Nights in a Bar-room* [1855] (Bedford, MA, 2000), p. 108.

7 Salvatore Calabrese, *Classic Cocktails* (New York, 1997), p. 7.

8 Joseph Lanza, 'Set 'em up, Joe', *Esquire*, CXXVII/4 (April 1997), p. 74.

9 Naren Young, 'Latino All-Stars', *Santé*, XII/2 (March/April 2008), p. 76.

10 John Doxat, *The World of Drinks and Drinking: An International Distillation* (New York, 1972), p. 148.

11 John F. Mariani, 'Manhattan Cocktail', in *The Dictionary of American Food and Drink* (New Haven, CT, and New York, 1983), p. 246.

12 John Burdett, *Bangkok 8* (New York, 2003), p. 273.

13 Robb Walsh, 'Texas's Margarita Miles', *Saveur*, 112 (July 2008), pp. 52–3.

14 Mariani, 'Margarita', in *The Dictionary of American Food and Drink*, p. 246.

15 Bill Ryan, 'Smirnoff White Whiskey – No Smell, No Taste', *New York Times* (Sunday Connecticut Edition), 19 February 1995.

16 Doxat, *The World of Drinks and Drinking*, p. 123.

17 'How the Moscow Mule Changed Cocktail Culture', at www.cocktailatlas.com, accessed February 2012.

18 Doxat, *The World of Drinks and Drinking*, p. 103.

19 Calabrese, *Classic Cocktails*, p. 122.

20 'Highball', Wikipedia, available at http://en.wikipedia.org, accessed May 2011.

21 Harvey W. Wiley, *Beverages and Their Adulteration* (Philadelphia, PA, 1919), p. 385.
22 Paul Clarke, 'Seeing Green: Absinthe is Back – Better than Ever', *Imbibe*, 11 (January/February 2008), p. 34–41.
23 'Energy Drink "Cocktails" Lead to Increased Injury Risk, Study Shows', *ScienceDaily*, 4 November 2007, available at www.sciencedaily.com, accessed February 2012.
24 Erik Lillquist, 'The Top 10 Best Energy Drink Cocktails', *MetroWise*, available at www.metrowize.com, accessed February 2012.

4 The Globalization of the Cocktail

1   Quoted in Barnaby Conrad III, *The Martini: An Illustrated History of an American Classic* (San Francisco, CA, 1995), p. 11.
2   John Doxat, *The World of Drink and Drinking* (New York, 1971), p. 102.
3   'The New Cunard Liner "Aquitania"', *Engineering*, 29 May 1914, p. 73.
4   The Cunard Passenger Log Book. Season 1902–1903. Royal Mail Twin-Screw Steamer 'Campania', p. 35, both at the Phillips Library, Peabody Essex Museum, Salem, Massachusetts.
5   Graham Greene, *Brighton Rock* (New York, 2004), p. 65.
6   ss *France* Press Release, May 1960, at the Phillips Library, Peabody Essex Museum.
7   Doxat, *The World of Drink and Drinking*, p. 18.
8   Ibid., pp. 65–6.
9   Jerry Thomas, *The Bartender's Guide; or How to Mix all Kinds of Plain and Fancy Drinks* (New York, 1876).
10 Doxat, *The World of Drinks and Drinking*, p. 74.
11 David A. Embury, *The Fine Art of Mixing Drinks* (New York, 1958), p. 118.
12 Salvatore Calabrese, *Classic Cocktails* (New York, 1997), p. 104.

13 Arrigo Cipriani, *The Harry's Bar Cookbook* (New York, 1991), pp. 13–17.

14 Christopher B. O'Hara, *The Bloody Mary: A Connoisseur's Guide to the World's Most Complex Cocktail* (New York, 1999), pp. 2–5.

15 Quoted ibid., p. 100.

16 The Woman's Union, *First Presbyterian Church Cook Book* (Kittanning, PA, 1941), p. 8.

17 Yoko Ogawa, *The Housekeeper and the Professor* (New York, 2009), p. 169.

18 Doxat, *The World of Drink and Drinking* (New York, 1971), p. 44.

19 O'Hara, *The Bloody Mary*, p. 75.

20 'Bloody Mary', at http://en.wikipedia.org, accessed February 2012.

21 'Caesar Cocktail', at http://en.wikipedia.org, accessed February 2012.

22 'Singapore Slings', *Oh Gosh*, available at www.ohgo.sh, accessed May 2011.

23 'Thomas Davey', Wikipedia, available at http://en.wikipedia.org, and 'An Explosive Cocktail', at www.Old Foodie.blogspot.com.

24 Lacey Griebeler, 'Latin Libations', *Chef*, LII/4 (April 2008), p. 17.

25 Quoted in Conrad, *The Martini*, p. 11.

26 Lisa Shea, 'The James Bond Martini Recipe – Casino Royale, at www.bellaonline.com, accessed 9 January 2008.

27 Tobias Steed and Ben Reed, *Hollywood Cocktails* (Minocqua, WI, 1999), pp. 16–17.

5 The Social Side of the Cocktail

1 Maud C. Cooke, ed., *The Twentieth Century Cook Book* (New York, 1897), p. 86.

2 The Woman's Union, *First Presbyterian Church Cook Book* (Kittanning, PA, 1941), p. 143.

3   The Cheshire Women's Club, *Recipes from Old Cheshire* (Cheshire, CT, 1938), p. 103.

4   The Marblehead Hospital Aid Association, *Sea Fare* (Marblehead, MA, 1958), p. 20.

5   Elmore Leonard, *The Hot Kid* (New York, 2005), pp. 191 and 264.

6   Ann C. McGinley, 'Babes and Beefcake: Exclusive Hiring Arrangements and Sexy Dress Codes', *Duke Journal of Gender Law and Policy*, XIV (2007), pp. 257–83.

7   Sotheby's, *Cocktails*, sale catalogue 7409, 30 September 1999.

8   Lucy G. Allen, *A Book of Hors D'Oeuvres* (New York, 1941), p. 4.

9   Ibid., p. 15.

10 William Grimes, *Straight Up or on the Rocks: The Story of the American Cocktail* (New York, 2001), p. xv.

11 Graham Greene, *The Comedians* (London, 1967).

12 Leslie Brenner, 'Cocktail Party', in *Encyclopedia of Food and Culture*, ed. Solomon H. Katz (New York, 2003), vol. I, pp. 424–5.

13 John Doxat, *The World of Drinks and Drinking: An International Distillation* (New York, 1971), p. 103.

14 Dara Moskowitz Grumdahl, 'The Cocktail Gender Divide', *Gourmet*, 15 November 2007, available at www.gourmet.com, accessed May 2011.

15 Heather Bouzan, 'Judgment Day – Local Bartenders Share What They're Really Thinking When You Order that Drink', *Stuff@Night* (Boston), 29 January 2008.

16 Quoted in Allison Perlik, 'Mock Trials', *Restaurants and Institutions*, CXIX/1 (January 2009), pp. 41–2.

17 'Molotov Cocktail', Wikipedia, available at http://en.wikipedia.org, accessed May 2011.

18 'Winter Cocktail Hits the Hub', *Metro* (Boston), 29 January 2009, pp. 1, 3.

19 Caroline Zimmerman, 'Britney Downed Toxic Cocktail Pre-Meltdown', *newser*, 7 January 2008, available at www.newser.com, accessed May 2011.

20 Chris Francescani, 'Anna Nicole Smith's Final Drug

Cocktail Ruled "Accidental Overdose"', 26 March 2007,
available at http://abcnews.go.com, accessed May 2011.

21 Mintel International Group Press Release, 'Mintel Serves
Up Restaurant Menu Trends for the New Year', Chicago, 9
January 2008, at www.mintel.com, accessed February 2012.

22 'Emerging Food Trends', *Catersource*, VI/1 (January 2008),
pp. 20–21.

23 Robert J. Benes, 'Shochu (show-chew)', *Chef,* LI/10
(October 2007), p. 14.

24 At www.theshochu.com, accessed February 2012.

25 At www.chinesemuurhilversum.nl, accessed February 2012.

26 A. Elizabeth Sloan, 'What, When, and Where America
Eats', *Food Technology*, LXII/1 (January 2008), p. 27.

27 Allison Perlik, 'Pour it On', *Restaurants & Institutions*,
CXVIII/1 (January 2008), p. 56.

28 '2009: A Year for Discovery and Value', *Santé*, XIII/1
(29 January 2009), p. 11.

29 Ibid.

30 'Cocktail Culture Meets Fine Dining', *Restaurants and
Institutions*, CXVIII/13 (15 March 2008).

31 '2008: Welcoming Choice, Value, and Service', *Santé*, XIV/1
(January 2008), p. 7.

Select Bibliography

Bullock, Tom, *The Ideal Bartender* (St Louis, MO, 1917) reprinted
  as *173 Pre-Prohibition Cocktails* (2001)
Calabrese, Salvatore, *Classic Cocktails* (New York, 1997)
Craddock, Harry, *The Savoy Cocktail Book* (London, 1930)
DeGroff, Dale, *The Craft of the Cocktail* (New York, 2002)
Doxat, John, *The World of Drinks and Drinking: An International
  Distillation* (New York, 1972)
Embury, David A., *The Fine Art of Mixing Drinks* (New York,
  1958)
Grimes, William, *Straight Up Or On the Rocks: The Story of the
  American Cocktail* (New York, 2001)
Lanza, Joseph, *The Cocktail: The Influence of Spirits on the American
  Psyche* (New York, 1995)
Miller, Anistatis, ed., *Mixologist: The Journal of the American
  Cocktail*, II (New York, 2006)
Reagan, Gary, *The Joy of Mixology* (New York, 2003)
Sismondo, Christine, *America Walks Into a Bar* (Oxford and New
  York, 2011)
Smith, Andrew F., editor in chief, *The Oxford Encyclopedia of Food
  and Drink in America* (Oxford, 2004)
Standage, Tom, *A History of the World in Six Glasses* (New York, 2005)
Thomas, Jerry, *The Bartender's Guide or How to Mix all Kinds of
  Plain and Fancy Drinks* (New York, 1876)
Waggoner, Susan, and Robert Markel, *Cocktail Hour: Authentic
  Recipes and Illustrations from 1920 to 1960* (New York, 2006)

Wisniewski, Ian, *Vodka: Discovering, Exploring, Enjoying* (New York, 2003)

Wondrich, David, *Punch: The Delights (and Dangers) of the Flowing Bowl* (New York, 2010)

Websites and Associations

The Museum of the American Cocktail
www.museumoftheamericancocktail.org
The first museum in the world dedicated to preserving and
celebrating the history and culture of the American cocktail.

Master Mixologist Dale DeGroff
www.kingcocktail.com
Dale DeGroff, often referred to as the 'King of Cocktails',
honed his bartending skills at great establishments, most
notably at the famous Rainbow Room in New York. He
is recognized for his gourmet approach to recreating great
classic cocktails and has invented hundreds of his own using
fresh squeezed juices and exotic ingredients.

Bartender Magazine
www.bartender.com
'First magazine for, by, and about bartenders.' Contains cocktail
recipes and information on contests and events.

International Bartenders Association (IBA)
www.iba-world.com
The IBA was founded in 1951 in the Saloon of the Grand
Hotel in Torquay, UK. Great archive of flair bartender events.

Extreme Bartending
www.extremebartending.com
All things that have to do with flair bartending.
Training, DVDs, resources, links.

Miss Charming
www.miss-charming.com
Extensive list of cocktail recipes, links to cocktail sites,
publications and organizations.

The Liquid Muse
http://theliquidmuse.com
Natalie Bovis-Nelsen is your guide through Cocktail Land.
She is creator and editor of this website, blog, online show
and serves as cocktail consultant and instructor.

Alex's Cocktail Recipes
www.cocktailmaking.co.uk
Extensive list of cocktail recipes and links.

Cocktail Times
www.cocktailtimes.com
Contains a cocktail dictionary, plus cocktail recipes and
recipes for foods to serve with cocktails.

Imbibe Magazine
www.imbibemagazine.com
The magazine of liquid culture. It looks at drinks as a distinct
culinary category, deserving in-depth exploration of history,
ingredients, preparation, artistry and consumption

Acknowledgements

This book would not have been possible if it hadn't been for the patience of Michael Leaman, the publisher of Reaktion Books, and Andy Smith, the editor and chief of the Edible series. Andy gave me the right amount of encouragement and technical advice when I needed it, always asking, 'When are you going to leave your day job?'

The draft would still be in the computer if my wife Harriette had not edited the manuscript, she says fifteen times. I don't doubt her for a moment. Her contributions are so significant she should be listed as co-author. She is a saint and I love her dearly.

My colleague and dear friend Jeri Quinzio, culinary historian and award-winning food writer, deserves my special thanks for reading a draft of my manuscript. She brought much needed insight and clarity to virtually every section of the book. Jeri, thank you and let's have a cocktail soon.

Special thanks to Historic New England for permission to use the image of *Devil Liquor* by an anonymous nineteenth-century painter which I discovered hanging in the pantry of one of their many historic homes. Some of my research was conducted at the Phillips Library at the Peabody Essex Museum in Salem, Massachusetts. They have an international reputation for materials on maritime history and New England life and culture. For a lover of books, time spent in their reading room was a joy. Additional research was conducted at the Boston Public Library and the Ipswich, Massachusetts, Public Library. I thank the staff of all of these libraries for their courteous assistance and support. Cheers to each of you.

Photo Acknowledgements

The author and the publishers wish to express their thanks to the below sources of illustrative material and/or permission to reproduce it:

Photos by the author: pp. 20, 24, 35, 42, 58; author's collection: pp. 10, 27, 29, 57, 59, 70, 81, 84, 85, 92, 95, 97 (ACME), 101 (APWire-photo), 103 (Herbert Photos Inc); Bigstock: pp. 38 (Catherine Laurin), 69 (Mark Stout); © The Trustees of the British Museum: pp. 13, 15, 28, 31 32, 41, 91; Dtarazona: p. 76; Courtesy of Historic New England: p. 21; Istockphoto: pp. 48 (Paul Johnson), 63 (3i-mediaphoto), 66 (Hulton Archive), 71 (Jill Chen), 73 (Ivan Mateev), 107 (mediaphotos); Library of Congress: pp. 12,16, 30, 45, 53, 86 top, 87; Magnum Photos: p. 88 (Cornell Capa © International Center of Photography); The Match Bar Group, London: p. 105; Raffles Hotels and Resorts: pp. 74–5; Rex Features: p. 86 bottom (Everett Collection); © 1992 Sandy Skoglund: p. 89; Shutterstock: pp. 6 (Bochkarev Photography), 47 (objectsforall), 67 (LLocQ), 68 (Andre Blais), 93 (Palmer Kane LLC), 98 (Palmer Kane LLC), 99 (Letizia Spanò); Stockxchng: pp. 64, 96 (Christoffer Vittrup Nielsen).

Index

italic numbers refer to illustrations; **bold** to recipes.